NORTHWEST of
the WORLD

Olaf   Swenson

NORTHWEST OF THE WORLD

FORTY YEARS TRADING AND HUNTING IN NORTHERN SIBERIA

by

OLAF SWENSON

With Illustrations

DODD, MEAD & COMPANY

NEW YORK   1944

A PATHFINDER BOOK REPRINT EDITION
Complete and Unabridged

Printed in the United States of America

ISBN: 979-8-8691-2402-9

ILLUSTRATIONS

NORTHWEST of the WORLD

CHAPTER I

IT WAS in 1900 I made my first trip to the Arctic. It was the first year in a new century, a year which seemed to have added significance because, instead of only twelve months lying behind it as a unit of time there lay one hundred years of the 19th century and the 20th stretched ahead, fresh and ready for new events. Since then, until recently, few years have passed during which I have not spent some time in the Arctic, either on the American or the Siberian side, and I have come to feel as much at home in a deerskin parkey as in an American business suit and much more so than I ever do in a dinner jacket. I suppose I have had as many friends among illiterate Siberian natives as I have among American business men and I know that I have found talk of walrus, foxes, and polar bears far more interesting than talk of the American stock market. And perhaps I have learned as much about people and about human life in general from these illiterate natives with whom I dealt for years as I ever have from my own race.

I was born in Manistee, Michigan, in 1883, at a time when the Great Lakes region, especially Michigan, Wisconsin, and Minnesota, was still rich with tremendous timberlands of pine and hardwood, magnificent forests whose green tops came crashing down to be made into lumber or paper at the merciless encroachment of the woodman's axe.

My father was both directly and indirectly engaged in reaping some of the harvest of the lumbering industry. He was financially interested in some of the timberlands but his business life centered around a hotel which he owned in Manistee and a large and prosperous saloon which was a part of it. And "Big Nils," as everyone called my father, dominated the saloon and the people which frequented it.

He was six feet, two inches tall and weighed over 260 pounds. I can remember the commanding figure which he invariably made striding into his own saloon. And if there was any suggestion of a challenge to his strength, he would reach back of the bar and pick up two ordinary oak beer kegs, grasping them by putting his fingers on the side of each keg and his thumbs over the top of the rims. Then with a grin and with no apparent effort he would lift them up simultaneously and set them on top of the bar.

Those were the days when a man's physical prowess, more than any other attainment, won him honor among his fellows, and Big Nils was held in high esteem and became almost a legend throughout Michigan. A promoter learned of his tremendous strength and asked him if he would fight John L. Sullivan; father, always ready for a good-natured fight, agreed although he knew nothing of professional boxing. A challenge was sent to John L. for a rough and tumble fight. But Sullivan refused, since he was willing to trust himself in the ring only when the contest was restricted by Queensberry rules.

Father was constantly engaged in one escapade or another, all in the spirit of good-natured fun. Not long ago I saw a picture of Diamond Jim Brady driving a horse and buggy into a saloon and I felt a momentary wave of jealous resentment, for this was one of my father's favorite tricks and I felt as though Diamond Jim had been stealing his thunder.

Big Nils had run away from his home in Sweden when he was fourteen years old. After spending a couple of years in Christiania (now Oslo), Norway, he came direct to America and went to Manistee.

Several years later he made his first trip back home, a surprise visit. He had prospered in America, had learned to dress immaculately in the American fashion, and when he reached the village in which his father still lived no one recognized him. He had planned this trip so as to reach home on his father's birthday, and when he got there he found a crowd of boisterous friends celebrating the day. Everyone was in good humor and no one bothered to wonder about the identity of any stranger who might come along and join the festivities, so that it didn't seem strange for Big Nils to mingle with them even though not a man there knew who he was. The whole party was several drinks up on Nils when he arrived. The men were testing their strength against each other, lifting weights, wrestling, twisting wrists, and pulling fingers.

Nils wandered into the house where he found his father seated at a table opposite a number of guests, successfully pulling fingers with them. One after another, his guests would fall before the mighty strength of their host. Then Nils sat down, and his father, joyfully facing the stranger, extended his hand, expecting to undo him just as he had undone his neighbors. Nils locked fingers with his father and with a mighty tug pulled the old man clear across the table. For a moment his father's face clouded with chagrin, and then suddenly a great light of joy came over his face and he came forward with outstretched arms.

"My God," he cried, "this must be Nils! There's no one else in the world could do that to me."

When Nils came back from that trip he had spent more than $11,000, which was big money in those days. A great part of the reason lodged in his big-hearted generosity. He felt so sorry for many of his townspeople, who were wasting away their lives in Sweden when the gates of opportunity were wide open in America, that when he boarded the boat to come back to the United States twenty of his friends were with him, all of whose expenses Nils paid.

We were a small and diminishing family. When I was six years old, my mother died in childbirth and her newly born baby followed her two weeks later. A few years after that another sister, two years younger than myself, was killed when she slipped and fell through an open hatch into the hold of a ship. Thus father, a brother two years older than myself, and I, were left alone and father never remarried although he was only thirty-two years of age when mother died. In his own childhood he had had a bitter experience with a stepmother which had caused him to leave his own home, and he said that he would never run the risk of making his two sons repeat that experience.

So instead of turning us over to a stepmother, he enlisted the aid of my grandmother with whom I lived until I was seventeen and who, at the age of ninety-eight, is still alive as I write this.

It was a good childhood and although, so far as I know, there were no seafaring men on either side of my family, the sea and the lure of exploration must have been in my blood even then. My favorite pastime as a boy was building small boats. I still have a big scar on my knee to mark the day when a chisel, which was shaping a keel, slipped, leaving the wood to plow into my flesh. I remember more vividly and painfully the sharp stab of the doctor's needle as he stitched it than I do that of the chisel itself and I can still smell the yellow iodoform which he put on it under the bandage; also I still have a vivid memory of my pleasure when the teacher sent me home from school because the odor of the iodoform was too offensive in the schoolroom. So I got a day's vacation.

I suppose it is natural that I should have carried in my own blood some of the instincts which were implanted in our family long before the memory of my father and his immediate ancestors. On one of my many visits to Sweden, I looked up the record of our family as far back as I could and found that my father had come from a section directly on the border between Norway and Sweden which had produced most of the old Viking kings. And in a place of honor in the house of an aunt of mine in Sweden I found an old bench with a high back that had been used by a Norwegian and a Swedish king centuries ago when they signed a peace treaty. But one of the most satisfying things that I discovered was a story about a pair of shoes which had once been worn by one of my forefathers and which are now carefully preserved in a museum on account of their great size. This comforts me whenever I have to go through the struggle of finding shoes big enough for myself.

In 1896, when the stampede to the Klondike was in full

swing, I was a tall, lanky kid too big for my clothes, with huge joints like those of a St. Bernard puppy, and I was itching for adventure. Everybody talked about the gold rush, and knowledge of the equipment needed for the expedition was as common as knowledge of the fittings for the kitchen sink. Excitement of this kind could not surge about Big Nils and leave him calm. He began to prepare to join the stampede and had an outfit practically completed when a building and loan association in which he was interested failed. Finding that he was unable to raise sufficient funds on his timberlands, he had to give up the expedition and we did not see the north that year.

Four years later, in the fall of 1900, my father, who had suffered considerably financially, became finally disgusted and left Michigan for Seattle, Washington, to start all over again. I joined him the following spring and at last we sailed for Nome, Alaska, on the trip we were to have taken four years before. Arriving at Nome, we pitched our tent along with hundreds of others on the beach, but during the night a southeast wind sprang up and the first thing we knew we were all thrown out of our blankets by breakers which rolled clear over our tents. We scurried to cover and the next day began looking for gold.

But we hadn't much success until we met a Swede who was a practical miner, and a church deacon from Spokane, Washington. The deacon had a claim a little way from Nome, and since he was cramped for funds he invited the other three of us to go in with him on a share basis, which we all agreed to do.

We worked about fifteen hours a day and I can still remember the stiffness of my fingers for the first three weeks when I would get up in the morning and find myself almost unable to button my pants. But to my surprise and delight I found that I could hold up my end of the work with the other men.

Yet, as hard as we worked, we were not making the fortune we had set out to find. The deacon, who acted as boss of the outfit, took charge of the clean-up, and whenever it came time to distribute shares it always turned out that the rest of us got only about ten dollars a day. We began to discuss the possibilities of an error in our settlements and the Swede miner hit upon the practical expedient of playing sick on clean-up day and watching the deacon as he weighed the gold. When he was all through and ready to distribute it, it seemed that a miracle had happened for that week each of us averaged about thirty dollars a day. From then on we had no trouble. With hard work and careful supervision of the result, we did well.

That fall we engaged passage on a two-masted schooner sailing for Seattle. The trip took us over a month and in that month I learned first-hand what it was to be really seasick. For several trips after that I invariably became seasick until one day, when I was standing on the forward deck of a boat with the sea rolling before me in a vast expanse and the wind threatening to blow a gale at sunset, it suddenly occurred to me that I was going to take a lot of sea voyages before I died, that somehow my work was going to keep me close to the sea most of the time, and that it was utterly ridiculous for me, a man now, who had chosen to live in contact with the sea, to be seasick. I have never been seasick since that day and on the basis of my own experience I now say that seasickness is ninety per cent mental.

The following spring father and I were back in Nome again, prospecting, and by chance it was here that we ran into the combination of circumstances which indirectly led me to my life work.

The Northeastern Siberian Company Limited, a mixed group financed by English, French, American, and Russian capital, had a concession for mining and trading in the northeastern part of Siberia, from the Anadir River to Cape North in the Arctic. The managing director was John Rosene of Seattle, and he was sending a group of fifty American prospectors from Nome to Siberia on a grub-stake basis. The company was to furnish transportation and whatever supplies were needed, and each prospecting group, made up of four or five men, was to stake out a 2,500-foot claim for themselves and a 2,500-foot claim for the company.

We were given lumber and tools with which to build boats, a large dory with sail for each group.

We embarked at Nome in the early part of July, 1902, and were landed at St. Lawrence Bay in Siberia. When our boats were completed, two groups, including the one of which father and I were a part, started along the coast headed for Kolutchin Bay in the Arctic, as we had heard rumors that this section was considered good prospecting territory. Our group consisted of four men: Bill Bissner, an ex-navy man who had had considerable experience in the Dawson country, a man named Louis, my father and myself.

About the third night out we were under sail with a strong fair wind close in shore near East Cape, immediately at the entrance of Behring Strait. Just as we were about to turn the Cape, we ran into a terrific cross wind which snapped our mast. Before we could clear away the wreckage and get our oars out, it was blowing a young gale. We were not more than 200 yards from the beach, so we began to pull for dear life to reach it; but when we got close we found the surf too heavy for us to land with our heavy boats. We then attempted to hug the land and return to Mud Bay, from which we had started, but the strong gusts of wind from the Cape were too much for us and we were blown out to sea.

All that evening and all night, until late the next afternoon, we bailed with a bucket and rowed like mad to keep the bow of the boat into the sea and, thanks to the good seamanship of Bill Bissner, we stayed afloat. That evening at last we landed, completely exhausted, thoroughly soaked, and with a healthy respect for both East Cape and the boats we had built.

But our introduction to Siberia was far from peaceful. We had been prospecting unsuccessfully for only a little while and all of the men were becoming impatient and disgusted with our lack of luck, when one day one of the men climbed a high cliff at Cape Serdge and found a huge collection of walrus tusks of excellent ivory lying there. It looked to him like a gift from God (instead of, as it actually was, something in the nature of an offering to God) and he came back bearing an armful of the tusks.

He was just coming into the camp when a couple of natives with a dog team arrived. When they saw the walrus tusks which he carried, they became furious. None of us knew much Chuckcha, their dialect, so we couldn't tell what they said, but we knew that they were plenty angry. We tried to talk in sign language and offered them gifts of provisions. Somewhat mollified, they finally took the provisions we offered, straightened out their dog team, and got ready to leave. Suddenly both of them made a concerted rush to Ericsson's tent, grabbed a watch and chain, and a knife which was lying beside them, ran to their sled, jumped aboard and were off like a shot.

Two of the boys started after them but the natives, when they saw they were being pursued, stopped their dog team and began firing with their rifles over the boys' heads; the boys, deciding that wisdom was the better part of valor, returned.

Since the Russian government at St. Lawrence Bay had refused us permission to have rifles, we were armed only with shotguns, and with natives hovering in the not too far distance and with us still ignorant of the real cause for their anger, we spent a sleepless night. Later, we learned that the tusks we had taken had been placed on the cliff as an offering to the walrus god to bring many walrus to the region. It is the custom all along the Siberian coast, where tusks are added every year to the rapidly growing supplies. In taking them, we had violated one of their religious customs.

Before daylight the next morning, in spite of the fact that a bad surf was rolling in on the beach, we were loading the outfits to go. We had had no luck here anyway and all of us half believed that the hills were crowded with natives waiting only for full daylight to take pot-shots at us.

Half swamped, we finally got away, wet from head to foot

and, giving the beach a wide clearance, we sailed along the coast, making about sixty miles that day. Finally, we landed again at a spot which we thought was far enough away from the angry natives to be safe, and went to work again. But once more we found no luck and, overstaying our time a bit in the fall in the hope that we would not have to return quite empty-handed, we got back to St. Lawrence Bay too late to catch the company's steamer and were forced to spend the winter there.

It was an interesting winter for me. I was the youngest member of the outfit and I learned a great deal from the old hands who had seen much of the world. We made out a set program in the fall and carried it out to the letter all winter. We had breakfast at eight o'clock every morning and lights were out at ten o'clock every night. The hours between were spent in playing football on the ice when weather permitted, playing cards, reading, and working walrus ivory into paper-knives, napkin rings, and so forth. I spent three months making a checkerboard, using walrus ivory and whalebone for the alternate squares.

It was during that winter, too, that I first encountered a typical death from Arctic cold. Three Russian boys had deserted from a Russian gunboat at East Cape. They hid in the hills until the ship had departed, then took refuge with the natives until the first of November, when, hearing of our camp, they started to come to see us. Before they got there they were all pretty weary from their overland trip and one of them, completely exhausted, lay down, saying he was unable to go further, although, without knowing it, he was within two miles of camp. He went to sleep lying there on the tundra, and the other two boys pushed on. As soon as they got to our camp, they told us about it and we hurried back to rescue their companion. But, although we traveled fast on their back-trail, when we got there we found him frozen to death. The other two boys stayed with us throughout the winter and earned their board by hauling ice which we melted for water.

Throughout the following spring and summer we went on prospecting for quartz, but without any satisfactory results. In the fall we sailed for Seattle. I was then only twenty years old, but I had had my taste of the Arctic and felt like a seasoned veteran. I knew that I would go back.

CHAPTER II

FOR a year and a half I worked as cashier and credit man for the American Biscuit Company in Seattle; but my feet, which had already become accustomed to the leaping deck of a small boat and the rough expanses of Arctic ice, felt restless and ill at ease under a desk. In the spring of 1905 they got into motion again. I knew a group of boys who had been in Siberia, and evening after evening we'd talk about a theory of ours that the mineral deposits on the Siberian coast directly opposite Nome must be the same as those found in the vicinity of Nome. Also, we were constantly tempted by the fact that the distance between the nearest points on the Alaskan and Siberian side was only thirty-eight miles, and that seemed to us more or less like an afternoon cruise.

When we talked to the Northeastern Siberian Company and found that they were willing to give us a concession on a territory about as large as the states of Washington and Oregon combined, we were filled with joy and optimism. We paid nothing for this concession and took it on the understanding that if we found gold on it, we were to get half the ground and the balance was to go to the company.

We left Nome hopefully in the motorship *Barbara Hernster*, headed for Anadir, the province which marks the northeastern corner of Siberia. There were twenty-nine prospectors aboard, besides a Polish trader named Count Lipinsky, and my wife and our six months old son. We had our own supplies, of course—provisions and mining equipment—including a large supply of dynamite. The general cargo consisted of a large stock of supplies belonging to the company which owned the boat; they had exclusive trading concessions in the territory to which we were going.

We had covered over half of our distance and were proceeding along the coast about half a mile off shore through a heavy fog, when the man on the fo'castle sang out to the skipper that there were breakers ahead. For some unknown reason the captain didn't take this announcement very seriously, and kept his course. A moment later there was a tremendous shock as though the ship had been hit forward with a thousand-ton sledge-hammer. Many of us were thrown off our feet and there was immediate confusion on board. Count Lipinsky began yelling "The dynamite! The dynamite!" and everyone, suddenly in a panic for fear the ship would blow up, rushed to the side.

The mate and five of the sailors got a boat lowered and got into it. But its keel had scarcely touched the water when an enormous sea hit it and smashed it to splinters, throwing all of them into the water. We fished them out and got the other boats safely into the water without drowning anyone.

Naturally, the first thing I did after the ship struck the reef and I had regained my footing, was to go to my wife and child, who fortunately were unhurt. I got them into one of the first boats to be successfully launched, was pushed in alongside of them, and, with the ship's engineer and a Russian doctor, we were the first to land, fighting our way through the heavy surf which threatened to capsize us at any moment.

When landing in heavy surf you don't pull the boat's bow into it, but turn and back in slowly, letting the bow of the boat rise on the breakers. My wife and I were sitting in the stern with our child and the Russian doctor was sitting in the bow. As we hit the first series of heavy breakers naturally some of the spray dashed over the doctor and he completely lost his head. Looking toward shore, he saw a welter of seething foam and I guess he suddenly thought he would be safer back on board the foundered ship, for he stood up, yelling wildly, endangering the lives of all of us. I don't remember what I said to him, but I know it was neither kind nor courteous; he suddenly collapsed, shaking violently, and half lay against the side of the boat. He never moved again until the boat grated on the beach and, lifted by a tremendous breaker, was thrown up onto the sand.

The next morning the sea calmed and the tide rose, lifting the *Barbara Hernster* slightly, so that, by setting sail on her, the crew could beach her, which they did. Meanwhile, we had set up tents and in as much comfort as we could find, were settling down to decide what to do next. All of our supplies were on the wrecked ship, of course, and all of the company's trading cargo, too. Everything was badly damaged by the water, but apparently a good deal of salvage was possible.

With the ship beached, I looked over the entire cargo manifest. The canned goods, of course, were still all right. The labels had soaked off of most of the cans, so that, hoping for a can of beans for supper, you might very well get tomato soup or apricots, but it was all good food. If you tried for beans and got plums instead, you just had to decide that you had opened a can of dessert first, and try again for beans —in which case you might get corn! It injected a certain amount of romance into the planning of a meal.

The trading company had a lot of pressed Russian brick tea, flour, and leaf tobacco aboard, and that looked pretty well soaked; but I prodded about a bit in it and then went to Count Podgorsky, head of the trading organization, and proposed that he allow me to salvage all of their supplies. I offered to pay the men who did the salvaging, and turn over to him all the non-perishable cargo—that is, the canned goods—if he would let me keep as my compensation all the perishables. Since he had no men and wasn't interested in salvage, he readily agreed, and I went to work.

I offered the prospectors who were with us a dollar an hour to work for me as salvagers, and put them and a number of natives to work building a wooden bin about twelve by sixteen feet and three feet high. Then we took the sacks of flour off the ship and dumped them into the bin, throwing aside the sacks with whatever flour stuck to them. When we had the bin full we washed and dried the sacks, sifted the flour, and refilled the sacks. We spread the leaf tobacco in the sun to dry and repacked it. The tea was all in bricks and wrapped so tightly that it wasn't hurt much. Of course, both the tea and the tobacco were a bit salty, but it was good tea and good tobacco in a land in which there was little of either.

When we got all through I owned a fine stock of real trading goods and didn't quite know what to do about it.

Meanwhile, the ship's engineer and two of the crew left for Nome, Alaska, in a whaling boat, for there was no wireless station nearer than that. It was like going next door to use the neighbor's telephone, only in this case next door was across 190 miles of rough northern sea. But they made it all right and after a while, in response to their message, a ship came along to pick us up and take us and our cargo on to Anadir, where we planned to look for gold.

On account of the Russo-Japanese War, Anadir was short of supplies, and soon word got about that I had a lot of flour and tea and tobacco. Flour was selling at $11 a sack, with sugar and other things in proportion. But I had no desire to be a profiteer, so I sold my flour at $1.75 a sack and had buyers from hundreds of miles around, who left with a comfortable feeling that they had been treated fairly.

In the late fall of that year we erected a station at Anadir and the boys went into the hills and began prospecting, while I, loaded down with flour, tea, and leaf tobacco, stayed at the station; I lived in a tent with my wife and child until the middle of November, selling supplies and getting acquainted with the country and the people who were to play such a large part in the rest of my life.

A group headed by Luke Nadeau, a French-Canadian, struck gold in paying quantities about twenty-two miles from our station. We could do no mining on any large scale, because we were not equipped for it, but in the spring we took out about $8,000 worth of gold, more as evidence that gold was there than anything else, and I took this to Nome, along with my wife and child, who returned to civilization while I went back to Anadir.

But by then I was convinced that there were other ways to make money in Siberia besides mining, and when I returned I carried a large cargo of trading supplies. The

Russo-Japanese War was still playing to a large audience, supplies were still scarce, and I did a thriving business.

We found plenty of gold, too, but just as we thought we had the world by the tail the Tsar's government stepped in and annulled the concession given to the Northeastern Siberian Company, holding that that company had no right to give subconcessions.

But it didn't matter much to me, for by then I was well established with the natives as a trader.

CHAPTER III

It was a bleak land in which I had chosen to center my business life for most of my active years, scantily populated and with little vegetation. There the cold northern sea beats thunderously against precipitous bluffs and capes or rushes madly up barren, sandy beaches flanked by lagoons. Inland, to the westward along the Arctic coast, the land flattens out and for fifteen hundred miles or more there is only the rough plain (which is called the tundra), and thousands and thousands of lakes.

The short spring and summer season begins in late May or June, though usually it is still possible to travel by sled in the latter month, if the trail is taken at night when the snow is slightly crusted. Toward the end of June the snow disappears rapidly along the coast, but by the end of August it begins to come again, at first in little flurries and then in blizzards which frequently last for days. The natives do not speak of the seasons as we do, but measure time by the movement of the sun. Throughout the summer season the long days are almost without night. But for two months, beginning in the latter part of November, there is no sun at all, and the natives speak of the time when "the sun will come back."

During the long winter, when the ground is covered with snow and ice, a strange light seems to envelop the land, especially at night. Distances are extremely hard to estimate and figures often seem distorted. Many a time I was fooled, especially at dusk. Sometimes, traveling over flat ground, I could have sworn that I was climbing a constant up-grade. Once I shot at a snowshoe leaning against a bush not twenty feet away, thinking that it was an owl. Another time in the spring I had my rifle raised to shoot at two geese, when suddenly I saw that they were two Chuckcho women, at some distance, swinging their arms which were covered by fur sleeves. One night when I was coming back into camp after a dog-sled trip into the interior, I passed our station and slept out in the snow less than a mile away, because I thought the lantern which the boys had hung out on a pole to guide me in was a star.

The people with whom I had cast my lot—that is, the natives of Northeastern Siberia—are called Chuckchos. They are divided into two main groups: those who live along the coast, called "Ankalin," and those of the interior, called "Chowchus." The coast natives exist largely by hunting sea mammals. Those who live in the interior, the deer men, subsist on large herds of reindeer.

There are many differences between them, easily distinguishable. The coast native is the natural trader; the deer man, the producer. In the old days they were as different as a New York stock broker and a western cowpuncher. Before the advent of the white trader the coast man was the go-between, dealing, for the deer man, with the whaling ships. In recent years, however, the situation has changed markedly and the deer men come in direct contact with the traders at the trading stations.

The deer men are entirely self-supporting. Reindeer furnish them with food and clothing. Nothing goes to waste, not even the entrails, the fermented stomachs, the blood, or the eyes, all of which they eat with relish. In the winter, when the reindeer are in corrals, their owners even squeeze the huge ticks from their backs and eat them with great delight.

Reindeer skins furnish them with every article of clothing which they use, from the soles of their boots to their hoods. The legs of the boots are made from the skin of the deer's legs, the soles from the hocks. The breeches, coat (parkey), and hood are all made from the skin of the body. The pants and parkey are made double, with fur inside and out. The socks are also made of deerskin. During the stormy weather a parkey of buckskin is added to this outfit, to keep the drifting snow out of the fur. The summer outfit is practically the same, except that sealskin boots and pants, which are waterproof, are worn instead of deerskin. Thread for sewing is made from deer sinew.

The women wear combination suits of double deerskin fringed with wolverine or wolf skin, if they are of the wealthy class, or plain dog if they are not. Long-guarded, well-furred, light-colored wolverine is highly prized, not only because it is fashionable but because the frost which forms from the breath is easily knocked off with a stick or reindeer rib from the long hairs of this fur, whereas it digs into any other kind, forming ice which cannot be brushed off.

Infants wear union suits of deerskin with mitts and boots attached, and with only a slit left in the crotch. A pad of moss, which is plentiful, is strapped on instead of a diaper.

Men, women, and children all chew tobacco. A chew of

tobacco is passed from mouth to mouth, and the native who does not offer his guest a quid of tobacco, even though it has been in his own mouth for hours, is a churlish host indeed. I have seen more than one baby in his mother's arms, yelling at the top of his voice, quiet down immediately when the mother took a chew from her mouth or from behind her ear and put it into his mouth.

A deer man's pipe is a work of art. It is made from an alder root, the bowl inlaid with lead and the mouthpiece made from an empty rifle cartridge. It is not considered of any particular value until it has become saturated with nicotine, and then it becomes one of the most prized possessions of its owner.

A native, before he loads his pipe with tobacco, tears a pinch of reindeer hair from the inside of his sleeve and packs it well into the bowl, putting the tobacco on top of it. Then he lights his pipe and pulls at it lustily, jabbing into the bowl with a little wire or bone poker. After a few pulls of tobacco and hair smoke he works up a good coughing spell, which seems to be his object. The harder the cough, the better seems to be the smoke.

The pipe is frequently of tremendous size and is carried in a buckskin bag made especially for that purpose and slung from the shoulder. I have seen pipes which weighed well over five pounds.

The coast natives like smaller pipes and have a weakness for pet-cocks from gas engines for bowls, and copper tubing for stems. If you have a gasoline launch near a coast village it is well to keep your eyes on it, else you may not be able to start it when you come back, because the men of the village have supplied themselves with new pipes.

Save at Cape Navarin, the natives do not build snow houses as they do along the North Alaska coast. The Karakees, who live at Navarin, seem a different sort of people from the Chuckchos, with various accomplishments which the latter do not have. They make beautiful pipes, splendid knives, steel spears, swivels, and other implements from steel, all of which are highly ornamental, and usually engraved and inlaid.

Karakee snow houses are permanent winter quarters and look like fortresses. They are made of snow packed about twelve feet high in a circle, and remind one of huge bass drums. Around the top of each house, stuck on poles, are the heads of dogs which have been sacrificed in religious rites and are kept to scare away the evil spirits.

To enter one of these houses, you go through a storm shed built of snow and down a long flight of iced stairs broken by several landings on which pillars of snow support the roof. When you come to the bottom you enter a tunnel about three feet wide by three and a half feet high, walled and shored up with driftwood. It is usually about thirty feet long and flanked by little rooms in which are kept dog feed, provisions, and this and that. Half way along the tunnel is a swinging door.

The natives manage to traverse this tunnel in a stooping position, but I found that it was all I could do to squeeze through it on all fours. Its purpose is to provide for defense in the event of attack by hostile tribes, or bears.

The inner room, or house proper, is about sixteen feet square and, like the tunnel, built of driftwood. In the center an open fire is kept burning, and there is a hole in the roof for part of the smoke to escape. The balance of it gets in your eyes and lungs, making short visits a necessity.

But the house of the Chuckchos is built of skins stretched on pole frames. It looks like half of a lemon with a hole in the top from which smoke escapes. The hut itself is called the *yarranga*. Inside it are usually several box-like rooms, made of skins stretched on ropes, called *yorrungas*.

The sleeping rooms are heated with seal oil lamps made of stone. In the olden days these lamps were of pottery, but the art of the potter has long been dead.

Nowhere are there any warmer houses, but the fetid air is beyond description! When a few natives have come in, taken off their clothes, and drunk many cups of hot tea, the odor is practically unbearable. Yet no matter how filthy, and lousy, and noisome a native house may be, it is the most welcome sight in the world to a traveler on a cold winter night.

And their hospitality is unexcelled. When traveling, it is not necessary to have intimate personal friends in the villages through which you are to pass in order to be sure of a place to sleep. When night comes and you pull into a village, you have only to go to the nearest *yarranga* and you are welcome.

Their religious life is largely a matter of legend and customs based on superstition. They have no formal worship. Yet it is amazing to find how many parallels there are between their beliefs and some of the stories of the Christian Bible.

There is a counterpart to the Noah's Ark story, for instance, in the story of the epic hailstorm sent by Ten-nan-tom-gi, the Great Spirit. This was before there were any animals in the Arctic, and the people were hard put to it to gain a livelihood. One of the hailstones which fell in this storm was of tremendous size and beauty, and the natives, attracted to it, began to work on it with their knives and shaped it in the form of a native hut.

About a month later they revisited the spot where it had fallen and were amazed to find how much it had grown. Again they worked at it, perfecting and embellishing it. And still it continued to grow, until it became the talk of the entire country; everyone passing nearby would visit it and, returning, report its ever-increasing size.

In the spring a number of natives came to see what would happen to the hailstone when the ice began to thaw. While they watched, it began to break up in huge crevasses and from every one came animals! Polar bears with white claws, brown bears, white and red foxes, seal, walrus, moose, and all of the other animals with which the Arctic is now populated.

The story would perhaps be less surprising if it used any other vehicle than a hailstorm, but, springing as it does from this, it offers an apparent analogy to the story of the flood, for in Siberia a great rain obviously would be a hailstorm.

The natives believe in one God and in a divine man who is an almost exact parallel to our Christ; a native who was perfect and who ascended to heaven, where he watches over them and gives them good hunting and peaceful death.

They have also an Adam and Eve—a first man and woman. The first man created everything which is useful:

the deer, the seals, the fish. The woman, on the other hand, created all that was evil: the wolf to kill the deer, the polar bear to kill the seals, the blizzards to kill the fine weather. Between them there is eternal conflict. When the man creates a fine day the woman works hard to bring about a storm; when the man sends seal, the woman sends along a Kaluchi walrus or polar bear to kill them. Because of this heritage it is inevitable, in native philosophy, that women should have worse dispositions than men.

The heaven that they have created in this primitive religion, is a place where there is always plenty of fish and game, and where the worthy go after death. The unworthy go there, too, but they are complete outcasts. When, in the next world, an unworthy one comes to a worthy one for shelter, he will be turned out; when he applies for food he will be denied, and will be compelled to roam the eternal wastes forever, hungry and without a roof over his head.

There are many rites and customs which undoubtedly have religious significance, though in many cases I think the natives who follow them do so only because they have been taught to, without any idea of why. When a deer man kills a deer he builds a fire, throws the tip of the animal's nose into it, smears some of the blood on his own face and on the faces of his children, and goes through a series of mystical motions with his hands. He believes that the smoke, ascending to heaven, will wipe out his sins. Here is an exact counterpart of the burnt offerings of the Old Testament.

When one of their number dies from a specific, localized ailment, the offending member will be cut away so as not to hamper the departed in the spirit world. If he dies of stomach trouble ("frozen stomach" they always call it) they will cut his stomach out. If he has been lame they will cut off one of his legs. There is no burial. The body is simply taken out onto the tundra and left there, with perhaps a few stones placed around it. Foxes or dogs gather after the funeral party has left and do the work of scavengers. It is not at all unusual to see a dog gnawing on a human skull.

There are very few old people to be found on the coast of Northern Siberia. The natives live to a ripe old age, but when they feel that they are becoming too old, so that they have become entirely dependent upon others, or are suffering from disease, they ask their closest male relative to send them to the happy hunting ground.

There are many ways of performing the ceremony. Where the people are not too prosperous, and where even bullets must be saved for game, the usual method is strangulation. Relatives and friends are called in, the departing member squats on the floor, one man on each side holding his arms, and the executioner takes a turn around the victim's neck with a rawhide string and twists, keeping the string taut until the twitching of flesh ceases. Then the body is taken out onto the tundra and left there.

In some sections you will find a rawhide loop always hanging from the middle of the hut, waiting and ready. Women are usually hanged, but sometimes a more prosperous native will honor his aging wife or mother-in-law by shooting her.

During my early days at Anadir a native named "Paganto" (which means "tie him up") worked for us. He was a well-meaning, gentle, tender-hearted person. He came to the station one day and wanted a new rifle, some calico, some sugar, some tea, and other similar goods. Since his credit was good I did not hesitate to give him all he asked for.

When he came to work the following day he seemed depressed. I asked him what the matter was and he told me that he had killed his wife, who was in the last stages of tuberculosis. It was for this, and for her journey to heaven, that he had bought the rifle and goods the day before. He had simply shot her, cut away her chest (the offending part) and placed the rifle and other things on the tundra beside her body.

A few months later he performed the same service for a demented woman whom we called "Fuzzy." He didn't buy a new rifle for her, but used an obsolete 45-70 Winchester. Since she was "all wrong" and he could not localize the seat of her trouble, he cut her up in several pieces before placing the remains on the tundra.

His mother-in-law still lived with him, but he was so poor now that it was difficult for him to support her. For a long time she pleaded with him to let her follow her daughter. Finally he consented, but felt that he could not afford another rifle. So he took his sticking knife and, thinking it might hurt her if he stuck the whole blade into her body, wound a rag around below the hilt so that only about two inches of the point were exposed. Then he chose a spot as near to the heart as he could and with one good push ended her worry and her dependence on him.

Within two years this good-hearted man, all within the spirit of his kindliness, had killed three women.

When a native and his wife are living alone and both die

at the same time through contagious disease, or are both strangled at the same time by their own requests, they are left in their house together and the house is never entered again. It simply stands there, with their corpses inhabiting it, until it falls from decay.

Of course it was a little hard to get used to some of these customs, but once you did they really seemed about as sensible as some of ours.

But I'll never forget the shock I felt during that first winter at Anadir when I found myself taking tea literally off the body of a dead woman. I was calling on some natives who were just taking tea and they invited me to join them. Of course the room was semi-dark, as it always is, since there are no windows in their skin huts, and the only light came from the stone lamps with moss wicks in seal oil. Tea was being served on a slab of wood which rested on something or other a little distance from the floor, with the natives sitting on each side of it. I sat down with them and was drinking my tea when the man of the house told me sadly that his wife had just died. I, of course, expressed sympathy and went on with my tea in silence. Suddenly the man pointed under the slab of wood and said "There she is," and I found to my horror that the wood was resting on her body and that my feet were actually pushing against the body as I drank. The strange part of this is, that while it might seem a sacrilege to us, the family was actually doing the dead woman honor by serving their tea over her body in this way.

During the same winter I saw the funeral, if you can call it that, of a girl of about twelve. Her body was brought out and put on a sled which was only about sixteen inches wide and a little tippy. The snow was quite rough at that spot and so, in order to keep the body from falling off the sled the man of the house simply straddled the corpse, with his feet on the runners, and drove away.

None of these things intimate any disrespect whatever to the dead. These are simply realistic, practical people who face philosophically whatever happens.

I have often been asked about the love life of the Chuckchos. The question is a little difficult to answer because there is so little that is spectacular about it. The man takes a woman and they live together as husband and wife, and they have children. Generally speaking, they are monogamous, although every man expects his wife to bear him a son; if she does not do so, the custom of the people completely recognizes his right to take another woman, and a third, and a fourth, or as many as are necessary until he gets a son who will help him with his hunting later. But the practical side of the matter is that if the husband claims his privilege in this respect, he does not cast aside his first wife, and the polygamous household seems to get on quite harmoniously.

Nor is there what we would call here any general sexual promiscuity. The Chuckchos seem to take sex as a matter of course and never get very excited about it. They have also found ways of eliminating some of the stimuli of promiscuity which exist in what we are pleased to call a more highly developed civilization. There is a special sort of arrangement which exists between some men by which, when they visit each other, they exchange wives. Or if for any reason one of the men is absent, the other man is not only welcome to come to his house and sleep with his friend's wife, but is even expected to do so almost as a part of the obligation of friendship.

It took me a long time to discover this because they don't talk much about it. I came on it quite accidentally through the acquaintance of a native of East Cape whose name, literally translated, was "Big Wind." He would often go walrus hunting with us on our boat and almost invariably, when he came, a younger man would be with him whom Big Wind asked us to take along, saying that he was "all same my brother." But there was no facial resemblance and I felt quite sure that they were not actually blood relatives of any kind. So I checked up on it and found out that the two boys, and the two girls who were their wives, had grown up together in the same neighborhood and that when they had married they had quite naturally entered into a reciprocal marriage agreement. When Big Wind went hunting alone for a couple of weeks, he would go to his friend's hut to announce his departure and to let him know that he would expect him to keep his wife company. When Big Wind's friend went away, Big Wind would do the same.

While it is an unwritten law that a man can take more than one wife only if his first wife bears no son, occasional exceptions are made in the case of natives who are wealthy. I know one native who had four wives although he had two grown sons by his first wife. All four of the women lived together with him in perfect accord. The first three were plain women well along into middle age, while the fourth was a young girl of dazzling beauty, judged by native standards. I asked him one day why he had married all of them, in view of the fact that his first wife had fulfilled her part of the bargain.

"Well," he said, "my first wife is a marvelous seamstress. My second wife is awfully good at skinning foxes and cooking. My third wife is very good generally around the house and my fourth wife—well, I just kind of like her."

Perhaps the greatest surprise which met me there was the discovery that homosexuality is not specifically the product of civilization. Male homosexuals are not uncommon among the Chuckchos and are quite as easy to detect as they are in Greenwich Village. They speak and dress like women and everything about them seems completely feminine. While female homosexualities seem less common, I remember distinctly one girl who not only acted and dressed like a man but, scorning the duller activities of women, went walrus hunting and in every way lived like a man. And in one of the villages I found a very ancient piece of ivory carving depicting two women quite obviously and intentionally drawn in the role of lovers.

In appearance, the Chuckchos are like the Mongolians and Japanese. They are small, with finely built bodies. The women frequently tattoo their faces, and of course, like their sex the world over, vary and decorate their dress in accordance with their economic and social status.

The men, like friendly children, love to get together for sports and gossip. Wrestling is their favorite sport and they take it seriously enough to go into definite periods of training for it. I have seen natives running in a circle half of the morning, holding a big rock first in one hand and then in the other.

They are good jumpers and their jumping contests reflect a good deal of the skill needed on the ice. Three mounds of sand, with a little stick on each one, are placed about eighteen inches apart. Then with a running start, the contestant tries to cross the three mounds, knocking the stick off with his feet as he goes, without disturbing the sand. This is purely and simply the result of the swiftness and nimbleness of foot which is necessary when crossing floating ice-packs.

It was into the country of these people that I went, now no longer a miner but a trader, depending for my livelihood upon a stock of staple goods which I had brought with me from America, along with a policy of fair dealing.

CHAPTER IV

IN ENTERING Siberia as a trader I was following in the paths of generations of others who were attracted by the richest fur crops in the world; in the early days they had gone into a country so wild and forbidding that scarcely anyone outside of it knew anything about it at all. The Siberia I encountered, even in its worst aspects, was tame and without hazards compared with what the first white men who invaded it had had to face.

Until the latter part of the 16th Century the great land now known as Siberia had no name, nor was any of it in the control of Europeans. It was known only as a wild, waste land inhabited by aborigines and tremendous numbers of fur-bearing animals. Daring traders, operating along its borders, had brought sable and sea otter, fox and other furs to the markets of Europe. Sable—the king of all furs, and the fur of kings—was so plentiful that a royal gift of sables would always consist of "forty forties" or sixteen hundred skins. Sea otter, predominantly a man's fur, was worn by aristocrats or merchant princes, and was a sign of rank. Today, both sea otter and sable are almost extinct and are protected by law.

Just as the white man was led into Alaska for gold, and into Africa for diamonds, so his lust for furs took him into Siberia. The priests and the law came later. Commerce and the lust for gold blazed the trail.

Even before any attempt was made to bring law to Siberia—even during the Tartar invasion of Russia which began in 1224—the great city of Novgorod was the capital of an independent and powerful republic, and the center of a great fur trade. Year by year its merchants, in their keen search for furs for the European markets, pushed ever eastward over the whole of Northern Russia, until they had reached a chain of mountains which seemed to them (after the dead level of the Russian plains) to touch the sky and to mark the limits of the world. Some called it the "Yugra" chain, others "The Stony Circle."

As their courage rose with frequent contemplation of the barrier, some of the more intrepid climbed and crossed the range; instead of the unbounded space of the universe, they found a land which in itself seemed apparently limitless, and this, like the chain of mountains, they called "Yugra." From this strange and distant land they brought back extravagant accounts of natives who were said to be speechless, and who lived like cannibals.

The Novgorodians never attempted to settle any part of the strange land, but were content to send marauding parties into it to barter with the natives and collect tributes of furs from them.

Meanwhile another stream of emigration, originating at Moscow, poured eastward. When Ivan III conquered Novgorod and annexed its possessions, he intercepted and stopped the Siberian trade of the Novgorodians. But the centralized government of Moscow was unfitted for the adventurous task of conquering unknown regions peopled by wild races. This was a job for men conditioned by the wild uncertainties of border life, and such a group of men grew up; nomads, some of them fugitives from the law, roamed the southern borderland, far from the reach of authority, secure in the liberty of the boundless plains. These men, without homes or families, were called Cossacks. Spreading over the waste borderlands, they advanced, driving back the wild tribes who disputed their passage, smoothing the way for settlement by a sedentary population. The role they played in the East was similar to that played by the trappers and backwoodsmen of early American history who, struggling against the Indians hundreds of miles ahead of American settlements, made possible the white man's expansion of the United States.

When the Russians reached the frontiers of the mysterious land of Yugra there was, among the settlers, a family named Strogonoff which had already acquired great wealth and influence. By the charter of Ivan the Terrible, the Strogonoffs were authorized to cut forests, colonize waste lands, establish salt works, and engage workmen. In exchange for these privileges, they were obliged to defend Russia from the incursions of the wild races beyond the Urals, and at their own expense they had to build block-houses, purchase guns, and keep up a sufficient armed force. The arrangement was a good one for both parties and persisted for three generations.

Meanwhile, another family—the Ermaks—was unwittingly preparing to produce a man who was to mark an epoch in the history of the world, one who was to become the greatest popular hero of Russia, though, strange to say, his name is hardly known beyond the frontiers of his own country.

The grandfather of this hero was called Ahhanasius Alenin, and lived in great poverty in the suburbs of Suzdal. Want of work obliged him to remove to Vladimir, where he became a drayman. At that time the dense forests of Murom were infested by bandits, and Alenin often transported them with his horses, being well paid for his valuable assistance. But this profitable business was of short duration. The complaisant drayman was arrested with a party of brigands and put in prison; however, he soon contrived to escape, and fled to Yurievetz Pobolski, a place on the Volga, where he died. His death plunged his widow and children into worse poverty. They heard of the flourishing business of the Strogonoffs on the river Kaina, of their demand for labor, and emigrated. The sons took the name of Pobolski from that of their last residence, married and had children.

Among the grandsons of the drayman of Vladimir, the most aggressive was Vassil. From his early years he was remarkable for strength and fluent speech, and when he attained manhood, his quick bright eyes, pitch-black hair, and thick, curly beard attracted attention in a community where physical qualities were the only marks of distinction. His first occupation was that of a tracker on the Kama and Volga. (Until the introduction of steam, vessels were constantly towed up stream by gangs of trackers.) His comrades bestowed on him the nickname of Yermak (the millstone of a handmill), a name which he made famous, and the only one by which he is known in history. The tame drudgery of a tracker's life soon disgusted the bold, adventurous Yermak, and he joined the Cossacks of the Don, who, struck by his daring, soon selected him chief of one of their small settlements.

He led his Cossacks to the Volga, where he gathered together a large band of robbers. His local knowledge now was invaluable. He knew the shores of the river and the habits of the trading vessels. Thus it was an easy task for him, perhaps not devoid of pleasure, to plunder the ships he had towed in his youth. The Volga was always a great commercial route. There was plenty of booty, and under a clever leader like Yermak, piracy flourished, to the terror and confusion of the traders.

At length complaints reached Moscow. Ivan the Terrible ordered that the pirates should be seized and hanged, and he sent an army to carry out the order. But Yermak was not there when the army arrived. Warned of their coming, he had fled with his band, up the Volga and the river Kama, to a wild, scantly populated district.

Some years before, as early as 1573, the Strogonoffs, enriched by their possessions on the Kama, had cast covetous eyes across the Ural to the mysterious and rich land of Yugra. They applied to Ivan the Terrible, and received from him a charter for Yugra similar to the one they had already received for the land on the Kama.

Now Yermak, a fugitive, proposed to the Strogonoffs that he lead an expedition into the new lands to conquer the natives and seize their territory, and the Strogonoffs, whose wealth enabled them to furnish the necessary arms and provisions for the distant and difficult expedition, readily consented.

With a force of 800 men Yermak started on September 1,

1581. Besides the Cossacks, he had a motley crowd of Tartars, Germans, and Lithuanians, whom the Strogonoffs had ransomed from the Nogai Tartars of the South. Interpreters were engaged, and even spiritual wants were not neglected, three priests and a runaway monk being attached to the party.

Yermak led his men up the river in a fleet of boats. They made slow progress, as they had to row against the strong current flowing between steep rocky banks. When the water grew too shallow for the heavily laden boats, it is said that Yermak dammed the stream with sails. But all of his local knowledge was of no avail; the boats had to be taken out of the water and dragged to the next stream.

A portage brought them to the small stream Jaravli and from there on they were in Asia. They floated down to the large Taghil and thence to the still larger river Tura, all forming part of the basin of the river Ob. On the river Tura the Cossacks were attacked by the aborigines, who shot arrows from the banks; but when Yermak's men discharged their firearms in return, the natives fled in great terror, imagining that thunder and lightning were being hurled against them.

The Cossacks then landed and sacked several villages, but were unable to capture any prisoners, as the whole population had fled. Later, when they reached the river Tavda, they succeeded in seizing one lone Tartar. Yermak, perceiving the impression produced by firearms, ordered one of his men to fire a musket at a coat of mail, which was pierced by the bullet. When the terror of the Tartar had subsided, he was questioned about the land and its inhabitants. He told them the whole country belonged to Kutchum, the Tartar chief who had invaded Yugra and conquered the aborigines, and who had put to death the envoy sent by Ivan the Terrible to demand tribute. His capital, Isker, or Sibir, was situated on the river Irtish. Kutchum, though old and blind, was a vigorous and tyrannical chief. He was assisted by a young kinsman, Makhmetkul, the most daring warrior of the whole region. All the surrounding tribes were subsidiaries to the Tartars, who were, however, unpopular, because they had tried to convert the pagan natives to Mohammedanism.

Yermak's position was somewhat similar to that of Cortez when he undertook his daring conquest of Mexico. His followers, though few, had firearms and defensive armor, while his numerous enemies fought with spears and bows and arrows. A quick victory was sure to break the power of the Tartars, as the natives were always ready to submit when they found a stronger master.

The Tartar prisoner was released, and, as was expected, reported to Kutchum the arrival of strangers with wonderful bows which shot flames and pierced iron coat of mail. Undismayed, the old chief hastened preparations to stop the enemy on the Tobol. In a place where the river narrowed, iron chains were thrown across the stream to stop the boats, and a large force was stationed on the banks to attack and destroy the Russians. A stratagem of Yermak's outwitted the Tartars. Bundles of sticks and brushwood were dressed up as Cossacks and placed in boats, with a few men to steer, while the bulk of the expedition landed and attacked the enemy on the banks. The Tartars, frightened by the numbers of the Russians advancing on all sides, fled without resistance.

This defeat obliged Kutchum to gather another and larger army to stop the invaders. It was divided into two corps. Kutchum, with the bulk of his force, entrenched himself at a short distance from the capital, while the cavalry, commanded by the renowned Makhmetkul, advanced against the Russians. The Cossacks were at first disheartened by the superiority of the enemy, who outnumbered them thirty to one, but Yermak encouraged them by his example, and a desperate engagement took place. Despite their numbers, the Tartars could not stand against firearms and were routed, but the victory was dearly bought, as Yermak lost many of his best men.

The Cossacks continued to descend the river Tobol, harassed by parties of Tartars shooting arrows from their hiding places on the banks. At last Yermak's men landed, and driving away the enemy, resumed their route on the river Irtish. Now they were near Sibir, and close to Kutchum, who had collected all his forces in defense of his capital.

On the morning of October 23, 1581, the Cossacks attacked the enemy, entrenched behind an abattis of felled trees, and a fierce struggle ensued. The Tartars surrounded their assailants on all sides; but the Cossacks, encouraged by Yermak and his lieutenant, Ivan Koltzo, who were everywhere in the thickest of the fight, resolved to sell their lives dearly. A lucky shot struck Makhmetkul, who had to be removed to the other bank of the Irtish, and the Tartars, now leaderless, were put to flight. Old blind Kutchum, hearing of the defeat, abandoned his capital in despair and fled south to the steppes of Ishim.

This victory, the most important they had won, gave the Russians the whole country from the Ural to the Tobol and Ob; but it cost the lives of many Cossacks, and many others deserted. Yermak now had but a few men left.

On October 26, 1581, Yermak occupied the abandoned capital of Kutchum, the town of Sibir. This name, which also applied to the surrounding country, was adopted by the Russians to denote their possessions beyond the Ural, and as these gradually grew until they reached the Pacific, so, by a common extension of geographical terms, the same word was used to indicate the dominions of the Tsar in Northern Asia.

Thus the name of a small Tartar town, the headquarters of an obscure chieftain, has become the collective geographical designation of the largest region on earth under one government. It is reported that in the town of Sibir the Cossacks found rich booty in silks, furs, and even gold, which was equally divided; but their newly acquired wealth could not purchase what they wanted most. Their provisions were almost exhausted, and as no food was found in the town, the near approach of the northern winter rendered their position very dangerous.

The news of the great victory, of the flight of Kutchum, and of the occupation of his capital spread rapidly among the natives, and as Yermak had expected, on October 30, the Ostiaks came to offer allegiance to their new masters. They also brought provisions and presents. The peace which now reigned over the country gave the Cossacks leisure to start fishing and hunting in order to collect a sufficient stock of food for the long winter. But their enemies appeared again, and in the beginning of December, Makhmetkul (having recovered from his wound) fell upon a party of twenty Cossacks, and all were massacred. Yermak had to leave Sibir in pursuit of Makhmetkul, who was again severely defeated and finally captured.

Now came Yermak's real triumph. Having completed the first part of his work, he decided that the moment had come to inform the Strogonoffs of the result of his undertaking. He realized the importance of his position, and he knew that the work which he had accomplished gave him great advantage. He not only wrote the Strogonoffs, telling them of his victories and of the capture of Makhmetkul, but he also sent a message to Ivan the Terrible, along with gifts, and with Makhmetkul as a prisoner of war. After asking pardon for his past misdeeds, Yermak added that the Russian Empire now had a new territory, the land of Sibir, which needed only the laws and the *voivodes* of the Tsar. The messenger charged with the delivery of this letter and of the prisoner, Makhmetkul, was the trusty lieutenant Ivan Koltzo, the robber chief of the Volga, who had been condemned to death by a proclamation of Ivan the Terrible.

The arrival of this strange embassy filled Moscow with wonder and pleasure. A handful of Cossacks had conquered the mysterious land of Yugra, and the wealth they had found was evinced by the valuable presents they had sent and the rich dresses of their envoys! The Tsar, who had shown displeasure at the departure of Yermak, was now soothed by the report of his success, and by the fine sables brought by Ivan Koltzo. He gave money and presents to the Cossacks and sent Yermak a fur mantle which had covered his own imperial shoulders. What was still more acceptable to Yermak was despatch of a *voivode* (an officer of military and administrative rank) and 500 *streletz* (foot soldiers).

The conquest of Siberia, even in the limited sense in which the expression was understood at that time, was far from accomplished. The forces at the disposal of Yermak were inadequate for his purpose as soon as the natives began to recover from the astonishment produced by the arrival of the strangers with their wonderful weapons. The powerful reinforcement sent from Moscow was of little use at first, because the *streletz* were less fit to endure privations than the Cossacks. The cold and moisture of the winter, and the want of fresh food, caused a violent outbreak of scurvy. The *voivode* himself and many of his soldiers fell victims to the disease, which raged until spring brought warmth and a supply of fresh meat.

A crafty Tartar chief, Karatcho, had won the confidence of Yermak by a specious show of friendship, and under pretense of seeking assistance, he enticed a party of Russians, including Ivan Koltzo, to his domain, where he treacherously murdered them. The news of this massacre gave courage to all the subject tribes, who revolted and laid siege to Sibir, surrounding the place with a long line of wagons, designed to prevent the exit of the Russians and to afford protection from their firearms.

But the courage of the Cossacks extricated them from this perilous position. On a dark night, June 12, 1583, led by Meshtcheriak, they stealthily penetrated the line of wagons and fiercely attacked the surprised Tartars, who were slaughtered in great numbers while asleep. The desperate struggle continued until the following midday, when Karatcho, finding he could not drive away the Cossacks from his train of wagons, fled to Kutchum in the steppes of Ishim.

During the two years since the Russians had established themselves in Sibir, commercial intercourse had been opened with distant regions of Asia, merchants coming even from Bokhara to barter their goods. A party of these traders had long been expected by the Russians, but now they were informed that Kutchum, their old enemy, had prevented the passage of the Bokharians.

Yermak, with his usual prompt resolution, started with a party of fifty Cossacks to meet the caravan, but after a day of fruitless search he was unable to find either the merchants or Kutchum. An encampment was chosen for the night with the deep rapid stream of the Irtish on one side, and a shallow ditch filled with water on the other; the boats were moored to the bank, the tents were pitched, and the tired Cossacks fell asleep. All were so exhausted that no watch was kept.

Unfortunately Kutchum was near. It was August 5, 1583, and the night was very stormy. The furious waves of the Irtish tore the boats away from their moorings and floated them down the river, and the noise of the howling wind and pelting rain drowned the sound of the advancing Tartars.

Old blind Kutchum had been informed that the Russians were sleeping but would not credit the report, fearing an ambush. A scout was sent with orders to find a ford across the ditch, to enter the camp stealthily, and bring back proof of the report. He returned with three muskets. The delighted Kutchum could no longer doubt that chance had given him at last an opportunity to have his revenge and destroy the terrible enemy who had deprived him of his dominions.

Amid the roaring of the storm the Tartar cavalry rushed into the camp and commenced the butchery of sleeping Russians. Only two were able to get to their feet—a Cossack, who escaped to convey the news, and Yermak. He fought for his life, but at a glance he saw he was alone and had no chance. He rushed to the river bank to find a boat, but the boats had all drifted away. Driven to bay, he plunged into the deep river, in the vain hope of swimming to the boats; but the weight of his armor dragged him to the bottom, where his body was found a few days later, clad in its rich coat of mail with a golden eagle on the breast.

Such was the end of the founder of the Russian Asiatic Empire.

The expedition of Yermak was followed by a stream of adventurers and traders. They penetrated first into the northern part of Siberia, to which the Russians were confined by the hostility of the warlike southern tribes. And even here they braved death and disaster in their search for furs.

There were two ways of obtaining these valuable furs from the natives. One was by trade, the other by collecting tribute which was paid in furs, as money was a thing unknown in those days in Siberia. All the conquered and subject tribes were obliged to pay tribute in furs, and parties of Cossacks were sent all over the country to collect them.

Traders followed, and in some cases even boldly preceded the official expeditions, bartering with the natives for the precious commodities.

Trade increased rapidly so that in 1640 no less than 6,800 sables were collected. There was such abundance of them that even the simplest Cossacks sometimes had coats lined with sables. The search was so keen, and the Cossacks spread so actively from every *ostrog*, that sometimes rival parties, starting from different quarters, met to collect tribute in the same locality, which often caused fierce quarrels. The ever-increasing demand, the growing numbers of immigrants all eager to acquire affluence, together with the diminishing numbers of fur-bearing animals, obliged the Russians to search constantly for new, unexhausted regions.

As the penetration of these roving bands southward was checked by the Mongol tribes (who didn't easily forget the time of Genghiz Khan), the Cossacks were forced to move eastward. The advance in this direction was also facilitated by the course of the rivers and the configuration of the country.

The collection of tribute (or as the Russians called it, *yassak*), as the Cossacks advanced, became robbery pure and simple, and though it was done in the name of the Tsar, probably most of the collected furs never reached the central government. Often the natives left their trapping grounds and moved out of reach of the Cossack bands. Again the furs played an important part. The government, realizing that the collection of the *yassak* would be greatly facilitated if they had the good will of the natives, began little by little to see that the promised protection became a fact, and that law and order were established in the acquired territory.

This process is still going on. The Russian proverb—"God is too high and the Tsar too far"—operated with terrible significance in Siberia. Still, perhaps on the whole, the fate of Siberian natives, notwithstanding the terrible cruelties of the Cossacks, has been slightly better than that of the American Indians.

The known history of Siberia is the history of the white man's search for furs.

When, in 1707, the Cossacks in Kamchatka, unable to bear the ferocity of Atlasoff (their commander) mutinied, they confined him in prison and confiscated his goods, which, according to the list, consisted of 1,235 sables, 400 red fox, 14 grey fox, and 75 sea otter. As these must have been collected during a few months, and formed only a small item in the government tribute, this shows how abundant furs then were in Kamchatka, and how ruthlessly the Cossacks had despoiled the natives.

Numerous other expeditions followed upon Yermak's and the penetration eastward continued until finally the Russians reached the Pacific. The Peninsula of Kamchatka was conquered in 1700 by Atlasoff. There was much rebellion among the natives. The conquest of Kamchatka marks the last stage of degeneration of the Cossacks who had been corrupted by their constant intercourse with the natives during a century's march across the continent.

The confusion in Kamchatka reached such lengths that in 1710 there were three commanders there—Atlasoff, who had escaped from prison, governing in the *ostrog* of Nizni

Kamchatsk; Tchirikoff, who had not yet given over charge; and Lipin, just arrived to assume command. The Cossacks, however, found ghastly means to solve the difficulty. Lipin was murdered in an ambuscade while on his way from Nizni to Verkne Kamchatsk; Tchirikoff, as he was returning to Yakutsk, was seized near the gulf of Penjina, bound and thrown into the sea. It was more difficult to remove Atlasoff, for he was feared as a dangerous man, so a treacherous plot was devised. Three bold men were sent with a letter, with orders to set upon him while he was reading it. But the messengers surprised him sleeping in his hut, and cut his throat without resorting to any stratagem.

Order was slowly established in Kamchatka only when communications were made easier. The northern peninsula, besides furnishing a new supply of furs such as sable, red, blue, and white fox, and sea otter, which was of special interest at the time, also gave Russia her first port on the Pacific—Petrapavlovsk—and indeed her only one, if we wish to be geographically correct, as both Vladivostok and Nikolaievsk are situated on the shores of the closed seas of Japan and China.

This long history of terror and bloodshed, of conquest and robbery, is the heritage of every trader in Siberia today. But now their hazards, in a land whose people are at last peaceful and hospitable and far removed from those warlike bands first conquered by Yermak, are reduced to those of the elements.

CHAPTER V

THE principal industry at Anadir and all along the north-
east coast of Siberia, the industry for which I was acting as
middleman, is trapping white foxes which are found in
quantities on the vast, bleak tundras and the Arctic floes.
There are two varieties of the animals, one which lives on
the land and the other which lives on the ice. The land fox
has coarser fur and is larger than the ice fox. It lives in
burrows in the ground, having several outlets in its den for
easy escape. For food it catches mice, an occasional ptarmigan, and in the summer it scours the beach for seaweed.

The ice fox takes his chances on whatever he can find,
following polar bears and rushing in when a polar has
killed a seal and is off guard; or, waiting until the polar is
through with his meal, in order to take the leavings.

White fox are not nearly so cunning as red fox and the
average native hunter can usually get at least twenty-five
skins in a season, if he gives a reasonable amount of attention to his work. I have known a single trapper to get as
many as a hundred with a line of fifteen traps.

Russian trappers with a long string of deadfalls will get
three hundred or more foxes in a good season.

His method (if he cannot locate a fox den) is to scoop
out enough snow to make a depression in which to place
the trap, covering it with a thin sheet of snow crust and
scattering bait of dried fish or meat over the top. No bait
is placed directly in the trap. Then he sets a stick in the

snow to attract the attention of the fox.

Finding a fox in the trap, he pokes a stick at it, which the animal seizes; the trapper then presses the fox's lower jaw into the snow, and jumps on the animal with his knees, putting steady pressure over its chest in order to suffocate it. A hard blow on the head would make the fox bleed and mess up the white fur, so that is carefully avoided.

Huge droves of mice venture onto the floating ice packs, furnishing the ice fox with food. Whether the mice are migrating from southern regions or coming down from unknown islands in the Arctic, no one seems to know; but of their existence there is no doubt. Both Russians and natives have told me of the thousands and thousands of mice that come ashore during the fall, sometimes swimming in open water between the ice pack and the land.

Although the principal catch is white fox, an occasional red or blue fox wanders into the traps of the natives, and now and then, though very rarely, a silver fox is caught. This, of course, is a tremendous event, since a single skin in the old days brought as much as $500 to $1,500.

There are wolves in this vicinity, too, but not anything like the numbers generally supposed. Wolf skins make by far the best sleeping bags for an extremely cold climate. But they are hard to get, for wolves do not abound along the coast, and those that are here are the hardest animals in the world to trap. They are suspicious and extremely cautious and never approach any object directly; they circle it and run zigzag to sniff the wind in all directions for any suspicious evidence before closing in.

They raise great havoc among the reindeer herds, a single

wolf often killing fifteen or twenty during one night for the sheer joy of killing. They seldom kill during good weather, unless virtually starving, but wait for a blizzard when they can run directly into the herd against the wind without giving the reindeer any hint of their approach.

Generally speaking, wolves are not dangerous to men. I have had wolves follow my sleds from time to time, but with one exception, they never came within rifle shot, and on this occasion I was not in a position to use my rifle.

My first attempt to get a wolf resulted only in having the beast laugh at me. It was during that first winter at Anadir. I started out to hunt seal at the edge of the flaw ice, sitting in a boat on top of a sled drawn by a dog team. About a mile from shore one of the dogs gave a yelp and the team started off like a shot. I looked ahead and saw a beautiful, yellow-tinged wolf facing us and apparently waiting to welcome us, for he made not the slightest move to get away.

The dogs simply went wild, and I was helpless. I sat in the boat and had my hands full to keep from bouncing out. I have been in a lot of rough seas in small boats, but this was the roughest boat ride I had ever encountered. I couldn't reach my gun. I couldn't use my brake stick, for the boat covered the sled, sticking out on all sides. I could only hold on and wait for whatever might happen.

The wolf waited, too, until the leading dogs were only a few feet off, then he jumped nimbly to one side and stood there laughing at us. The dogs made an abrupt turn, the sled broke up with a jar, and over we went, I lying on the ice with the boat on top of me, and the dogs, a tangle of mouths, tails, and harness, trying to break loose to get at the grinning wolf. I pulled myself out just in time to see one of the dogs in the middle of the team bite through the tow-line, and the four lead dogs, held together by the harness, tear off in the direction of the wolf.

The wolf seemed only to want to play, apparently sensing the great disadvantage under which the dogs labored on account of their harness. He zigzagged in front of them, and when he got too far ahead of them, he would wait until they got close to him before starting off again. As far as I could see them, they kept up this game.

The following morning the dogs returned completely exhausted, with the tow-line missing and their harnesses chewed to pieces. I suppose they had become badly tangled up in their harnesses, and before they chewed themselves free, the wolf, at last tiring of his sport, had gone about his business.

One morning during that same winter I saw a wolf about a mile off shore. At once I went into the bunkhouse and shouted the news, whereat six of the boys came tumbling out with their guns and we all started taking pot shots at him. It was a long range for good shooting, but we could see where our bullets hit the ice and changed our ranges accordingly. The wolf just sat there and looked at us, which was strange behavior indeed.

Suddenly he let out a yell, indicating that he had been hit, but still he didn't try to get away. Three of the boys shouted in chorus, "I hit him," and we all started toward him. A hundred yards off we stopped and fired another volley. This time the animal dropped. As soon as the first man got there—one of those who had clamored the most loudly that it had been his shot which killed the wolf—he disclaimed all responsibility. "That wasn't my shot!" he cried. The others joined him with like denials.

The "wolf" was only a poor, scared, lonesome dog, who apparently had become separated from his team and was trying to find a new home. None of us felt very proud of our marksmanship that morning. Some of the sled dogs have a wolf strain in them, with the same color and general appearance, and at a distance are undistinguishable from a wolf.

Wolves in the north seem few in number and seldom appear in the ordinary course of events, but the natives tell me that a polar bear or brown bear can bring them out in quantities by invading a wolf's lair and devouring the young. In such an event, the mother wolf will travel over the tundra with a peculiarly mournful howl, and wolves will gather from all quarters to take up the trail; when they have tracked down the bear, they kill it.

Occasionally you will hear of an attack made by a wolf on a man or dog team. A native told me of one occasion when his team was attacked between Chaun Bay and Kolimsk. The wolf came up behind the sled, having passed four other teams, and sprang upon his lead dogs. The driver killed the beast with his knife.

If a wolf attacks a native who has no gun and the man has enough presence of mind to hold out his cap with his left hand (or, better still, his skin shirt if he has time to get it off), the wolf will lunge at the object and the native can strike with his knife in his right hand.

If, on the contrary, the wolf leaps before the native is

prepared, the beast will usually seize the man's wrist or arm and prevent him from drawing his knife.

From the sea, the natives get seal, an occasional whale, and walrus. Sealskins are perhaps the best money crop, but the walrus are plentiful, too, and can furnish the natives with ivory for trading, meat to eat, and skins for their houses and boats. There are two different classes of walrus: the smaller, clam-eating variety and the larger *Kaluchi* which live on seals, fish, and clams.

They are apparently not of two different species but only creatures of different habits and the product of chance and environment. The *Kaluchi* is almost always a large bull, the forward part of whose body is covered with scars of many combats. The native theory is that he is an abandoned walrus who, as a pup, has been segregated from the herd and thus been forced, through circumstances, to fight his way alone, eating whatever he could find, or gaining his food by conquest in order to subsist. Those which survive naturally develop a fighting instinct far above that of the average walrus, and will attack and kill seals, sea-lions, and even polar bears. A *Kaluchi* is shot on sight, even though the native knows that he will not be able to retrieve the carcass, for as long as one is around there are no seals. As soon as the walrus is shot or driven away the seals reappear.

Among the most dramatic battles in the Arctic are those between walrus and polar bears. The attack is made by the bear, who will creep up behind a walrus (usually a cow or a pup) and if he is able to reach his prey before the latter slips into the water, will slap a paw over its hind flippers. This is not easy, for the walrus, always wary of the approach of man or beast, usually lies within a few feet of the water, often with its head or tail right at the water's edge, so that it has to do little more than shift its weight to slide quickly and silently into the sea and disappear. When the walrus lie in herds (which number from six to two hundred), there are always two or three constantly on the lookout, as if posted on guard, and the approach of an enemy is a signal for the whole herd to take to the water.

But, assuming that a bear gets one paw on the flippers of a victim, his next move is to deal his prey a terrific blow across the back with his free paw. Frequently, this one blow will break the back of the walrus. At the very least, it completely knocks the wind out of him and causes him to throw his head backward or to one side, whereupon the bear seizes his upper lip or throat, and the battle is soon over. Frequently, when the bear's hold is on the upper lip, it will tear the entire lip and scalp off the walrus in one jerk.

The bear isn't always victorious, however. As in football, the advantage is pretty apt to be with the contestant on whose home ground the battle is waged. If a *Kaluchi* walrus catches a bear in the water, the victory is a quick one for the walrus. He simply clamps the bear with a vise-like grip between his front flippers and goes to the bottom.

One native told me that he had actually seen a walrus haul himself out of the water to attack a polar bear, take him bodily between his two front flippers, drag him off the ice, and dive into the water to carry the bear to a quick death.

In another case some natives were hunting in a skin boat. At some distance they saw a polar bear feeding on a seal.

Paddling carefully, silently, zigzagging to keep ice between them and the bear, they approached within shooting distance. But just as they were about to fire there was a commotion in the water at the edge of the ice cake and a huge *Kaluchi* stuck his tusks over the edge of the ice right under the bear's nose. The bear let out a stentorian roar and rose to attack, but the walrus kept right on coming, never stopping until he had his front flippers hard around the bear's barrel, stabbing savagely with his tusks which were driven by one of the most powerful necks in the world.

Assaulted by the terrific jabs of those tusks and held by the ten-ton squeeze of those flippers, the bear could do little with his jaws. He could only try to keep his head out of the way, protecting it as best he could with his forepaws, while the claws of his hind feet tore savagely at the walrus's belly.

Exhausted finally, the latter let go of the bear and started to drag himself painfully toward the water, leaving the victim of his attack writhing in agony on the ice. Then realizing that he was not being pursued, the walrus apparently changed his mind and started back toward the bear, but couldn't quite make it. When the natives got to the ice cake they found both bear and walrus dead, the bear's head crushed to a pulp and the walrus with his entrails hanging out through a great rip in his inch-thick skin. Not only did the natives witness one of the most terrific battles which nature can stage, but they got a fine polar bear and a huge walrus without having fired a shot.

In my opinion, walrus hunting is the sportiest hunting in the north. The average man who had not tried it would say that failure to get a walrus, once one was sighted, would indicate very poor marksmanship. But many things besides marksmanship enter into it. In the first place, the quarry has unusually keen senses of smell and hearing and must be approached carefully up-wind. All unnecessary noise must be eliminated and the boat must be kept out of sight behind ice. There is little chance of success unless you are at comparatively close range, for the skull of a walrus is an inch or more thick and there are only two spots—one between the tusks when his head is raised, and the other at the back of the head, each about three inches square—which a bullet will penetrate fatally, and then only with metal-cased bullets.

When you have come close enough to a herd to shoot profitably, the entire herd is almost sure to be in motion and there are so many heads bobbing up and down before your eyes that it is with difficulty you can connect your sights with one of them long enough to pull a trigger effectively. Added to this, if you do shoot one near the water's edge, he will almost certainly drag himself into the water and sink like a brick. A shot in the body accomplishes nothing at all, for the body is like a huge sack of grain and the bullet simply imbeds itself in a mountain of flesh without even seriously inconveniencing the mountain.

Once, aboard our *S.S. Belvedere* on a walrus cruise, our ship's engineer became sarcastic about the fact that I had returned from a walrus hunt without a walrus. He had never hunted them but considered himself an excellent shot.

Annoyed at his persistent heckling, I made him a bet. He

could pick his herd, his weather conditions, his time, his natives, and his firearms, and under the most favorable conditions he could assemble, I bet him ten dollars that he would not get a walrus.

He took the bet avidly—it would be like taking candy from a baby, he decided—and waited for his chance. One fine day he sighted a lone bull fast asleep on a cake of ice. The weather was fine, all of the conditions were in his favor, so he decided to collect his ten dollars.

Using great caution, he approached to within a few yards of the walrus without waking it, and raised his gun. With any marksmanship at all it looked as though he would win without any trouble. But just as his finger contracted on the trigger his boat shook as though it had been hit by a tidal wave, and took a decided list to port. His gun went off in the air, the bullet doubtless passing a hundred yards above its mark, and the engineer had to hold on to the gunwale of the boat for dear life to prevent a ducking in the Arctic Ocean.

What had happened was the result of a strange coincidence, too unlikely for fiction, but which sometimes comes about in real life. Another walrus, which had been at the bottom feeding on clams, rose for air just at that moment and ran into the boat on his way up.

Naturally, I collected the ten dollars, for by the time my friend had regained his balance, both walrus were far away from there.

The proper method is to pick out a large bull and, if he ducks his head before you shoot, keep your sight on him until he again raises his head. If you shift to another, that one will almost certainly duck his head before you can pull the trigger and you will simply be bobbing from one to another and never get a shot before the whole herd is in the water.

There is comparatively little danger in hunting walrus. The young bulls, with tusks about six inches long, are the most vicious, and at times do not hesitate to strike at the boats, but they are fairly easily routed. A herd of cows with young will sometimes surround a boat, but a few shots will scatter them in a stampede, the young "pups" hanging to their mothers' backs by their flippers, and getting a swift ride through the water.

There has been a great deal written about polar bear hunting, but I would just about as soon hunt dairy cows in a pasture. As a rule the poor beasts are terribly frightened at the approach of a man and haven't a chance in slack ice where a ship or skin boat can easily out-maneuver him. I have never heard of a healthy bear charging a man in the open. I have seen two or three which were mildly curious, but when one of the men went "shush" at them, they were off like a shot.

In the old days, when natives hunted bears with lances, it was quite a different matter. The only part of a polar bear vulnerable to a lance is a spot directly below the throat, and if the lance missed that the native's only recourse was to outrun the bear. Consequently, only the best sprinters specialized in bear hunting.

Killing a bear under the circumstances created by native custom (which, of course, means native law) is often an ungrateful job. The man who sights the bear gets the skin, no matter who kills the animal. Also, if you borrow a gun and happen to kill a bear with it, the bear belongs to the man who owns the gun. In that case the one who kills it is given a share of the meat and is entitled to the privilege of cutting off a bit from the end of the bear's nose for "good luck medicine."

Some years ago I bought a polar bear skin from a native, but the skin was practically ruined, since almost the entire head had been cut off. After we had agreed on a price I asked the man from whom I had bought it what had happened to it. He told me that he and another native had seen the bear at about the same time. They pursued the animal and killed him, whereupon a bitter argument ensued. Each native claimed the bear under the unwritten law of "My-bear-I-see-'im-first." They had finally made a compromise, ceding the bear to the man from whom I had bought the skin but providing that the other could cut off the tip of its nose. The other native, still angry, had acted the dog-in-the-manger, letting his knife slip to cut off almost the entire head so that the skin would bring a very low price.

Natives are funny about their bears. A man once came aboard with six polar skins. I offered him a high price for the lot, but he would not accept it. After considerable argument I tried another plan and began bargaining for them one at a time. I bought the first five skins without any difficulty, but on the sixth the man's demands were out of all reason. No matter how much I offered him he wanted more.

I had thought that I knew something of the ways of the native mind, but I could not seem to get to the bottom of this man's reasoning at all. The skin was no better than two or three of the others which I had bought at logical prices, and I knew that the man knew skins well enough to realize this, yet he refused an offer of twice as much as I had paid for any of the others.

Annoyed, I finally gave up and asked him to tell me where the "medicine" was in this bear. Thereupon he launched into a long story about how he had got the skin. He had gone off on the ice and been caught in a bad blizzard in which, for days, he had suffered cold and hunger. Finally, to cap the climax, he had got his finger in front of the gun when he had shot this bear and had blown the end of it off. Hence, he must be paid a great deal for the skin to compensate him.

I really couldn't muster any good arguments against his reasoning, so I paid him his price and closed the deal.

If one really wants grizzly and brown bear hunting, Kamchatka is the place to get it. I have seen as many as nine bears there in a day. Podproogin, one of Kamchatka's best hunters, killed sixty-five bears during a four day hunt in 1925. But the champion of them all is Severin Karlson, a Swede who has lived in Kamchatka for forty years. I believe that he has killed more bears than any other man in the world. I asked him once how many he had killed during the time he had been there and he said that he didn't know—he hadn't kept count after the first two years, during which period he had killed 726! It is hard to believe that unless you have hunted in Kamchatka and have seen the number of bears there. During the early years of my trading the annual export of bearskins from that section was from 3,500 to 6,000.

Karlson loves to tell stories about his bear hunting. Here is one of his best:

He and two Kamchadahls on a hunting trip had just made camp for the night and Karlson went to a small creek to get a pail of water. He was just about to fill his pail when he heard a sound from across the creek, and looking up, he saw a huge grizzly about sixty yards away. It was standing up facing him and offered an excellent shot. Karlson dropped his pail, seized his gun and fired. He was so close that he could hear the impact of the bullet on the bear's chest. The huge animal fell to the ground, but a moment later got to its feet and lumbered off.

Karlson crossed the creek, put his ear to the ground, and listened. For some time he could hear the thud-thud of the bear's feet upon the earth for it was in the fall and the ground was frozen. Then suddenly the sound stopped. Heading along the trail which he thought the bear had followed, he only went about three hundred yards before he came upon what he had expected—a bear lying quite still on the trail, his huge head on his forepaws.

Karlson set his gun against a bush, took out his knife and whetstone, and prepared to skin the bear. Leaning over, he gathered a good handful of its back skin in his fist. But just then things went off schedule, for the bear, with a roar of surprise and fear, suddenly made a high jump which was rivaled only by Karlson's. Dashing for his gun, the hunter swung and fired again, and this time there was no doubt that the bear died.

But Karlson had had enough of bear for the moment. Besides, it was almost dark, so he went back to camp. In the morning the Kamchadahls went with him to skin the animal. They found only one bullet hole in the skin, and that in the back—obviously from the second shot. Now Karlson was absolutely sure that his first shot had been a hit, so he left the natives and began circling the territory to see if he could find an answer to the riddle. In a few minutes he found it, on another little trail which led from the river— the carcass of another bear, with a bullet hole in its chest as evidence of the fact that his first shot had landed just where he thought it had. When, the night before, he had laid hands on that other bearskin he had been trying to skin a perfectly healthy, live bear which was simply taking a nap!

Grizzly and brown bears are very amusing creatures. Once, on a hunting trip in the interior of Kamchatka, floating down the Voroskoi River in a dugout canoe, during the early spring salmon run, I saw a bear fishing. He was sitting on a sandbar in four or five inches of water. When a salmon came within reach, swimming with its back out of water, the bear would put his two paws over the fish, give it a squeeze and lift it out of the water. Then he rose from his haunches, put the fish under him, and sat down again. He caught five salmon, but with the fifth between his paws, he seemed to sense something wrong and, standing up, and still holding the last fish he had caught, he turned around and looked at the place where he had been sitting. Not one of the other fish he had caught was there. Each time he had raised his haunches to put another fish under them the current had, of course, washed away the last one he had put there. With a growl of disgust he threw his last fish into the water, left the stream, and lumbered away into the brush.

On the same trip we saw another bear who had more patience and used his brains in a somewhat similar situation. His method was different from that of the first bear. He scooped out the fish, one at a time, using one paw to give each fish a terrific wallop that made it fly ten or fifteen feet over the bank, landing behind a little hummock.

I crept up quietly behind the hummock, without letting the bear get wind of me, and retrieved three fine fish he had already thrown there, thus getting an excellent dinner without effort. Then I retired and watched him again. Apparently desiring to gloat a little over the fish he had already caught, the bear came over to the bank a moment later and began looking around for them. Finding none, he looked about with evident surprise, but instead of giving up, he went patiently back to his fishing. This time, however, as soon as he had thrown a fish onto the bank, he followed it up, found it, and immediately buried it in the loose sand.

After that, I decided he deserved to keep whatever he caught, and having all the fish we could eat for supper, I went along and left him in peace.

Native trappers tell me that a brown bear will build a dam across a small creek when fishing, leaving only a small outlet through which the fish can come. A hungry bear will eat the entire fish. If he is not hungry, or if fish are plentiful, as they are at the time of the salmon run, he will eat only the head. The gristle-like part of the salmon, directly above the nose, is the part the bear likes best.

A brown bear depends a great deal upon his front paws

and is careful to keep them in good shape. This is why he does almost all of his digging with his hind feet, the claws of which are always worn short.

Kamchatka is full of bear stories. Here is one more: A native at Kolyutchin Bay, taking a nap on the beach, was wakened by a bear shoving its nose in his face. Having presence of mind, the native held his breath and waited for the worst. But the bear, after a few sniffs at him, and a few punches in the ribs with his snout, evidently decided that the man was something both unedible and unseemly, for the big paws began to scratch sand over the prostrate form of the man and in a few moments he was completely covered. Then, apparently feeling that his hygienic duty had been done, the big beast went peacefully on his way.

But not all bears are harmless. At Cape Saglasky, during a blizzard, a polar bear entered a native house, killed nine dogs which were chained in the outer house, and entered the sleeping room. No one was at home except a woman. She succeeded in cutting a hole through the skin wall, crawled through it, and went to the house of another native, who returned with a gun and killed the marauder.

CHAPTER VI

I BEGAN my career as a full-fledged trader in Siberia with considerable hope and some misgivings. My hope was based upon the fact that I believed in fair and intelligent treatment of the natives and felt that this would gain their cooperation by comparison with the treatment which they had received at the hands of the old-time traders. My misgivings were based upon my lack of knowledge of the people and even of the language they spoke.

Thinking ahead to the problems I would meet in Siberia, I decided that conditions were very much the same as those in northern Canada and Alaska and that goods which would be useful in the northern part of North America would be useful there. So in getting together the merchandise for trading, I bought dry goods, for instance, which would be especially appealing to the natives and had everything wrapped in packages of uniform size, first in waterproof paper and then in oilcloth and burlap. I did the same with flour, sugar, pilot bread, and so forth. Each package was made so that it would fit nicely onto a sled in the winter time or could easily be put into one of the pack-sacks which the pedestrian Chuckcho carries on his back. As nearly as possible, the packages were all of the same size and value and, of course, always had in them exactly what I guaranteed them to have, as to quality, quantity, and value. The natives were completely out of touch with the outside world. They had absolutely no way of determining the actual value of what I gave them save through comparison with what another trader would give them, and I knew that if I dealt with them unfairly in one season I would not get their furs the next.

There are many instances of traders who cheated the natives only to ruin their own futures. In some cases, of course, innocent traders suffered from the malpractices of others who had gone before them.

I remember especially a poor Russian of that region, whom I shall call John. For two seasons in succession he had had bad luck with American traders. During the first season, John came down to the coast with a fine lot of furs, and met an American trader who made him an offer. At first John refused because the price was so low, but he finally weakened and sold the furs. Later he met some natives who had traded with me and found that they had received about three times as much for the same number of furs.

The next spring John met another American trader who offered him a fine price for his catch but told him that he didn't have enough merchandise or cash with him to pay for the whole thing at the moment, but that he would take the furs with him to Nome, Alaska, and bring back the payment a few days later. Of course he never returned, and John began to have a pretty low opinion of all American traders.

The third spring, John—pretty cynical by now—came down to the coast with his furs and hunted up a Russian trader who was there. As it happened, it was near the end of the season and the Russian, although he was a perfectly honest man, was actually out of funds and merchandise. Quite innocently, he told John that he would be glad to take his furs, setting a good figure, but was sorry he didn't have enough with him to pay for them on the spot. If John would let him take the furs along, he would bring back payment in a month or two.

All of the bitterness of the two successive seasons in which he had been cheated flamed up in poor John at this point, and without a word he hit the Russian trader on the jaw, knocking him out. The trader must have been the most surprised man in the world when he came to, because he had been completely innocent and honest and had no knowledge, of course, of the events behind John's resentment.

The Chuckchos are very clever at bartering and it took some little time for me to get acquainted with their methods and thus learn how to deal with them. Before they ever brought their furs down to trade they had two or three months in which to carefully inspect and appraise them to decide just how much they were worth. These people have a tremendous amount of patience and will frequently prolong an argument with a trader throughout half a day. Naturally, unless the patience of the white man is equal to their own, he gets nowhere at all. I learned very early in my dealings with these natives that one of the most effective things that I could do in trading with them was to pick up a book or magazine in the middle of one of their long harangues, sit down and begin to read. If they see that you are in a hurry to close a deal, they know that they are winning. If they find that you have as much patience and time as they, you are pretty apt to win your point.

When the natives first came to me, during that first year at Anadir, I was determined at the outset to win their confidence. This seemed to me to be the most important thing, even if I might lose a little on a few deals. So I started out talking to them in sign language and in the few words of Chuckcha which I then knew, and I let them set their own prices. I laid out all of my supplies and gave them to understand that they were to take what they thought their furs were worth. Surprised, each native would come in with his furs, put them in a pile on the floor of the trading station and then go over my stock of merchandise, taking a package of flour here, a package of calico there, some cartridges, some sugar, and some tea, and lay them on top of the skins. When I would signify that I was satisfied with the trade that they suggested, they were tickled to death, and I honestly believe that I wasn't gypped once that winter. And when they got all through, I usually made them a present of some cheap thing, a knife or a little tobacco, or a pot or pan for each one to take home to his wife.

Later, the more I knew them, I learned that they really loved bargaining and that I could get along with them better by arguing a little. The trick, I found, was to argue with them until you had secured the furs for a little less than their actual value and then, when the deal was closed, make up any difference between what you had given them and the real value of the furs by giving them a present. I always saw to it that they were fully paid for their furs, but a part of the payments came in the form of a voluntary gift from me and I always tried to keep myself well supplied with the things they wanted most, both as actual payments and as gifts.

There was a Russian trader at Anadir that year who had a tremendous stock of Russian brick tea of which the natives are particularly fond. It is made of sweepings from the factory and pressed into bricks, packed eighty to a basket. I had run out of tea, and since this Russian had a surplus of it, I bought a rather large supply from him. He had been trading quite fairly, giving the natives a case of tea for four white fox skins. I at once began trading a case of his tea for five white fox skins. Yet I soon used up the supply I had bought from him and had to buy more. Bit by bit I used up his entire stock of tea and he never did understand why I could dispose of it when he could not.

The reason was very simple. It is quite true that I asked for five skins for the same amount of tea which he dispensed for four, but when the deal was all over and closed, I would invariably make the native a present up to the value of the other skin, giving him, say, a cup and saucer, some tobacco, a knife, some needles and thread, a few toys for the children and a chamber pot for his wife. I actually made a better trade for myself than the Russian did, but the natives would go home and recount at great length all of the things they had got from me for only five white fox skins, and all of their friends would remark on my generosity. Whereas they thought that the Russian, who gave them only a case of tea for four white fox skins, was very stingy indeed.

The Chuckchos are great beggars. They must have presents. They keep begging and begging until the white man is near to the end of his patience and if he would be successful with them he must be as long-suffering as Job. At the last minute they can think of a dozen things which they must have. They want a little lunch to eat on their trip home. They want a few more pieces of sugar. They want a little tobacco. They go wild with joy at the acquisition of little things.

They came to the station usually in groups, traveling with deer team or dog team. Some of them were on the trail for as long as six weeks in order to get to our trading stations. There was always one politician in the group, usually the chief of the little village from which they all came. He would invariably trade first or last and the trader had to get acquainted with him and learn what was his pleasure. He had to be paid a little more and be treated with a little greater deference, because he was the big chief. If he traded first and did not like the outcome of the deal, he would march out of the station with the others at his heels and there were no more dealings with that group.

Sometimes the natives were very cagey about revealing their catch. In the early days of that first winter a group came in accompanied by a Russian doctor, and a Cossack who acted as interpreter. They told me that the natives had only three or four foxes. One at a time, I bought four skins and each time the natives would go out in a group and come back with another from their sleds. When the day was over, I had bought fifty-four fox skins from them. Before coming into the post they had hidden all but the original three or four skins on their sleds, trying out my fairness with one skin after another until they had finally disposed of the lot.

Another thing which I had to get used to was their primitive system of counting. They counted everything they received by units of five. It was impossible to make a deal by giving a man eighteen or nineteen cases or boxes or packages. It had to be fifteen or twenty. As a matter of fact, it was actually easier to make a deal with fifteen packages than it was to offer nineteen for the same merchandise. They count up to ten and after that they say ten and one, ten and two, and so on, until they get to twenty. They express forty, for instance, by saying two times twenty.

This is also true among the Eskimos on our own continent. I remember selling two reindeer skins to an Eskimo in Nome. He asked me what I wanted for them and I said $14.00. He said, "No, I'll give you $15.00." I said, "But $14.00 is all they are worth and all I want." He said, "No, I'll not give you $14.00, I'll give you $15.00." Finally I said, "All right." He smiled at me and gave me $15.00. I smiled right back at him and gave him back a dollar as a present and everybody was happy.

One of the first and greatest difficulties which I encountered was an attempt to master the dialect of the Chuckchos. I thought I had been getting along beautifully but I soon discovered that I really knew just enough to keep myself in perpetual confusion. One day some natives arrived from Cape Navarin. After we had finished trading and I had fed our visitors I asked the customary question *Rapungel?* meaning, what news?

At first their story was the usual dull recital of the whereabouts of various natives, of how many foxes they had killed, etc. Then one of the natives began telling of a ship-wreck. The more he told the more interested and excited I became.

It seemed that an American whaling ship had been crushed by ice off Cape Navarin and all of the crew except two men had perished in their attempt to reach the shore. One of the survivors had had his feet so badly frozen that they had cut them off and he died. The other man lived.

We had thirty prospectors living with us that winter and I immediately called them together and told the story. After discussing the pros and cons for awhile we decided to send several dog teams to rescue the one remaining white man from the ship. Several of the men began to get sleds and sup-plies ready for the trip. While they were working I turned to the natives again.

"Just when did this shipwreck occur?" I asked.

Two of the natives sat on the floor in order to answer me. They each held up both hands, with their fingers spread wide, and pointed also to their feet. The shipwreck, about which we were all so excited, had happened forty years be-fore!

Later I checked the story up and found that it was all true. The sole survivor had been held by the natives and treated virtually as a slave for two years before he had been rescued.

During the same season we were stationed for some time at St. Nicholas Bay and were without coal, due to the fact that the ship which had brought it out to us had landed it at St. Nicholas Station, quite some distance from us. On account of this we were forced to scour the country for wood. We had been hauling it from the Russian Spit, about twelve miles from our station. Had we known that we would be without coal we would have gathered a supply in the early fall, as the natives did, before the snows were so deep, stacking it where it would be easier to get at.

As winter advanced and the snow got deeper, it became more and more difficult to find enough to keep our fires going.

One day two of the boys arrived at the station with loads of wood accompanied by a native from the Russian Spit, who came to me and delivered himself of a long string of gutturals. But I could only understand the last two words —"gummine cotoot"—which meant "my wood."

Now I knew that this native had a lot of wood collected on the spit and I could only assume, from his long harangue and the two words I could understand, that he was telling me the boys had taken wood from his woodpile. I suppose the suggestion came to me from the fact that I myself had been rather tempted by his magnificent collection on a day when I had helped in the arduous job of digging a load out of the snow; I couldn't really blame the boys much if they had done a little pilfering.

But I called Charlie Johnson, one of the boys on the sled, and asked him if he had taken wood from this fellow's pile. He said no, whereupon the native said emphatically, "Yes." Then the conversation developed into a monosyllabic argument between the native and Charlie. The more loudly Charlie shouted "no," the more the native bellowed "yes."

Finally Charlie had enough of it and, taking the native by the nape of his neck and seat of his skin pants, tossed him into a snowdrift. But he was up in a moment and back again, a pleading note in his voice. I began to suspect that there was more in what he said than had met the ear, and urged him to speak slowly and say it all over again. When he did, I saw that Charlie and I had been acting like ungracious dolts.

"Please take my wood," he pleaded. He had seen what difficulties we had encountered in getting wood for ourselves and had come all the way to camp to offer us his.

The natives are reasonably honest and as soon as I learned to weed out the exceptions to this general rule I got along with them without any trouble. Sometimes, however, fate got in the way of the carrying out of their honest intentions.

A Kamchadahl, from Markovo, a settlement about 500 versts up the Anadir River, arrived at our station with an ordinary run of furs which I bought from him. After we had finished our business he told me of a silver fox he had at home and asked for about $200 worth of goods on credit, on the understanding that I was to get the fox and we were to arrange the exact price of it after I had seen the skin. I checked up on his story and found that he had the fox and that it was, by all reports, an unusually beautiful skin, so I gave the man the merchandise he wanted on his oral assurance that he would bring the skin down the river after the breakup in the spring.

The winter passed, the spring came, and with it the people from Markovo arrived at the mouth of the river. But the man who had agreed to bring me the silver fox skin was not with them. I asked about him and learned that he had been drowned. His neighbors were laconic about it and spoke darkly of his death, as though they were leaving something untold, something which it might not be good to hear.

Less interested in the story than in the skin I had bought, I asked them about that. Oh, the skin had been saved and taken in charge by the government who would sell it at auction in the interests of the man's estate. I went, of course, to the local government and told my story, but without result. There was no record of the transaction I had made with the man who owned the skin. The government was acting as trustee for the estate and had no choice save to sell it at auction and realize as much from it as possible.

I could not possibly have any objection to the logic of their position, so I swallowed my loss of $200 as gracefully as possible, without losing interest in the skin. Arriving at the auction, I found that a large lot of miscellaneous goods in which I was not interested would be put up before the fox skin and, since I was rather busy, I went away, after arranging with one of our customers to bid up to $250 for the skin when it came up.

Later in the day I learned that the silver fox had been put up and sold to my man for $240, but that afterwards one of my competitors had blocked the sale by bringing up the technical point that the man who had bid for me had no power of attorney to do so. Had he bid for himself there would have been no objection. The government ceded the point, put the skin up for sale again, and sold it to one of the Russian buyers for $240. The purchaser later offered it to me for $400, but by then I had had enough of that skin.

I suppose, as a matter of fact, it was partly superstition. By this time the silver fox had become a matter of current discussion among the natives, and though I hadn't then learned what it was all about, I knew that they thought something evil was connected with it.

It was not until after the Russian buyer had departed with it that I learned the story.

The Kamchadahl who originally owned it—the man with whom I had dealt for it, and who had been drowned before he could deliver it—had been working for a trader at Markovo, hauling freight during the winter with a dog team which belonged to the trader. On one of his trips, during a heavy snowstorm, a fox, running before the wind with his tail in the air, ran head on into the dog team. One of the dogs jumped the fox and held him until the driver killed it with his brake stick.

Now the unvarying law of the north is "my dog, my fox." Plainly the fox belonged to the man who owned the dog team. But the driver, when he picked it up and saw that he had a beautiful silver fox, worth what was to him a fortune, simply placed the carcass in a sack and said nothing to any of the other drivers or to his boss.

As soon as he got back he told the trader he would like to take a week off to go trapping. At the end of the week he astonished everyone by coming back with a prize silver fox skin. He told one of his friends and after his death the story leaked out. The superstitious natives, of course, immediately explained his death by the "evil spirit" which was in the fox skin—the same evil spirit which had made the man forget the law of the land and take what was not his.

And so, when the skin was later sold in Vladivostok for $650, I did not feel too badly about the profit I had missed, for by missing that I had also escaped the evil spirit.

But there was another native who came to me and asked how much I would advance him on a silver fox skin. Naturally I asked him about its size, its color, and its condition. Without hesitation, he told me that it was an unusually large pelt of a beautiful color. I asked him where the skin was. He looked at me with wide innocent eyes in which there seemed to be surprise at my question.

"No catchee him yet," he said. "By and by catchee him."

CHAPTER VII

Bit by bit I got acquainted with the Chuckchos that year and learned to like them and feel definitely that they were my friends. Many and many a night, when I was on the trail through the interior, I had reason to be grateful to them for their flawless hospitality. Their fare was poor and badly served and their houses invariably filthy, but whatever they had belonged to their guests, and this seems to me to be the measure of hospitality the world over. Sometimes their entertainment had its amusing side.

Once, when I made a visit to Barronkorf Bay, a native official made a formal call, asking me to go to his house for a visit. He was proud of the fact that he had been in the service of the government for a number of years and his breast was covered with badges which he wore as proudly as though each one were a cross of the Legion of Honor.

He had a log house, the most imposing in the village, and it was a palace, according to the native standards. It was large, clean, and airy but scantily furnished. As soon as I passed through the doorway he proudly led me to his best chair and insisted that I sit there and nowhere else. It was so conspicuously placed, so obviously commanding a view of the opposite wall, that it was apparent I had been seated thus for a purpose.

Then, as I looked along the wall, I saw why he had put me there. Directly opposite me, hanging prominently on a peg, was a red rubber fountain syringe, its tubing gracefully

A Yakut from Yakut's Republic, Siberia

draped over other pegs in a lovely serpentine course. He had picked it up somewhere, and was so proud of it as an evidence of his cultured position in the world, that he must use it as a decoration, and displayed it where all, especially white men from the west, could see it.

I became acquainted, too, with the practice of medicine men and this came about, strangely enough, through the experience of a white man whom I shall call George. George had a native wife. I had known him for some time, but meeting his wife for the first time, I noticed that she seemed depressed and tired, and looked ill. I asked him if she were well. He looked at me rather sheepishly and was hesitant to answer. Finally he did, but without much conviction.

"She had an operation yesterday," he said.

I was astonished and told him so. I didn't know that there were any doctors in the neighborhood and asked him where he had found one.

"You probably won't believe it if I tell you what happened," he said, still obviously embarrassed.

I urged him to tell me anyway and he went on. He said that his wife had been ill for a long time and finally, having heard a great deal of talk about native medicine men, he sent for one, telling him that the woman was suffering from "nan-kin-ya-katelin," which, literally translated, means "frozen stomach."

At this point George suddenly changed the subject and began talking about the fur catch that season, obviously regretting that he had said anything at all about the medicine man. I brought him back to the subject and he looked at me almost pleadingly.

"I don't like to talk about it," he said. "It sounds too ridiculous. No one would believe me."

"Go on with your operation," I urged.

Well, it seems that the doctor had told the woman to take off her clothes, which she did. Then he had her lie on the bed and he began examining her abdomen, gathering some of the flesh into one of his hands so that it looked as though there were a lump the size of a hen's egg directly under the skin.

"There is the trouble," the medicine man said, turning to George. "Have you a knife?"

George said that he had only a pocket knife and it wasn't very sharp, but the doctor grunted with satisfaction, said, "Nomelkin," which means "good," and reached for the knife.

Without further explanation, the doctor made a lunge with the open blade and apparently drove it up to the hilt in the woman's abdomen. Blood spattered in all directions, but the woman seemed to be suffering no pain. Then the doctor put his mouth to the wound and a moment later raised his blood-covered face and took out of his mouth what seemed to be a large piece of bloody flesh.

"What shall I do with this?" he asked.

"What the hell do I care?" George answered him, by now thoroughly frightened and disgusted.

So the native doctor put it back into his mouth and swallowed it. After washing the wound with water, he passed his hand over it a few times then called George to look. There was not a scratch to be seen anywhere.

Of course I laughed, but George was serious.

"I tell you I stood right beside him," he declared. "He couldn't fool me. I'm positive he jabbed that knife right into her stomach!"

The funny part of it was that the woman got well after that!

The natives, of course—at least a great many of them—believe implicitly in the efficacy of these medicine men. But this is easy to understand when one comprehends their nature. They are like simple, innocent, believing children. They are great literalists and they accept what their eyes tell them. I remember a reindeer man who came down from the interior and for the first time encountered a mirror in the trading station. It was a large glass and hung directly opposite the spot where he sat. Before sitting down, he had merely glanced at it and doubtless thought that all which he saw reflected there was simply an extension of the room in which we were. He stared in astonishment for a moment and then exploded:

"Ko-lo nemang-kin jarranga!" he grinned. (Which you might translate as, "Gee whiz, what a big house!")

Then he sat down, and this brought him directly opposite the mirror so that he saw his own reflection there.

"Yettee," he said courteously, which is the native greeting meaning literally, "You come."

There was no answer, but the native was not going to be offended by a slight taciturnity.

"Mankoyettee?" he continued, meaning, "Where did you come from?"

There was still no answer and with wrinkled brow, the native turned to another, saying, "It's funny. I see the man's lips move, but I can't hear him speak."

Never before having seen his own reflection, he had not recognized himself in our mirror.

One of our greatest difficulties at first was to keep the natives from breaking the glass in our windows in order to crawl through. They could not get used to the idea of a door which would shut or open as you wished, or to holes in the walls through which you could see but which went "crash!" when you walked through them.

One night I was wakened from a sound sleep by strange noises on the floor. I lit the lamp and looked around the room but could see nothing. Still the pounding went on. Then I went out and looked under the house. There was a native trying to get in. Encountering a white man's house for the first time, he had started underneath and tried to work upwards.

Incidentally, these entries were for no dishonest purpose. The most hospitable persons in the world themselves, the natives simply assume that they will receive the same hospitality from strangers. But they are always nonplussed, and either childishly delighted or scared half to death, by the things with which the white man surrounds himself.

And they cannot understand any suspicion of dishonesty or any safeguards against them. A white trader built a house at Anadir and put a padlock on his door. It was years before he could get any native to enter his house. They had been insulted by his locked door.

Before the first year was over, however, I discovered that on occasion the Chuckchos can be just as dishonest as any white man. Usually, though, it is in small ways. I knew a native who stole a file from me and returned it six months later, saying that his conscience hurt him. And another time we were lying at anchor aboard a ship off North Head. A part of the crew had gone ashore in a whale-boat to get water. They seemed to be taking a long time about their errand, so I went on deck with a pair of binoculars to try to uncover what was keeping them. As I looked, I saw that the crew had all gone up to one of the huts and the beach was deserted except for one lone native who seemed interested only in gazing at the sky. He would stand and look upward for a moment and then, with a slow, deliberate pace, walk a few feet, stop, and begin sky-gazing again. Then I noticed something on the beach, twenty-five feet or so behind him. Whenever he moved, the object behind him moved also. It took me five minutes, during which the native had moved a hundred yards, to discover what it was all about. And when I did, I got a megaphone and hailed the crew in the village. The native had attached a long rawhide thong to one of the oars of the whale-boat, and, step by step, was dragging it away with him.

Another time I was aboard a Russian steamer and saw a native get away with something like 200 pounds of loaf sugar, by making several trips to the shore. He had been sitting on a case of the sugar and found that there was a large hole in the cover. Quietly pulling one arm in through the wide, loose sleeve of his parkey, he worked down under the garment and packed the loaf sugar into the loose folds of his clothing. Casually he left the boat and went ashore. After a while he was back, sitting on the box again, only to depart when he had another load. It took him all day, but bit by bit, he emptied the box.

I remember only one instance in which a native deliberately stole some of our supplies in plain sight of all of us. He was a tramp whom I had taken in and fed up for a couple of weeks. Early one morning he appropriated a small light sled of mine, cut a slit through the large tent which served as a warehouse, took a sack of flour, some tea, some cartridges and a couple of packages of drygoods, threw them on the sled and started pulling the sled across the tundra.

I happened to go into the warehouse a few minutes after he left. I saw what had happened and immediately took up the chase. But as soon as I got within sight of him I realized that it would be a hopeless chase, for he could run like a deer and he more than kept his distance from me. When I had to pause for breath, he would stop to sit on the tundra, and turning his face toward the sky, would let out a weary, mournful howl like that of a wolf. By the time he had done that two or three times, I resented his hooting at me so much that I completely forgot the theft of the goods and was determined to catch him simply for the satisfaction of giving him a whipping.

I went back to camp, hitched up a team of fast dogs, got one of the other men and we started after the thief. About eight miles from our station was a high range of mountains and we saw very soon that the native was making for the highest peak. While we were still well down the slope, he reached the top. Here he stopped for a moment, sat on his sled-load of booty, alternately looking down at us and turning to howl at the sky. Then hitching around, still on the sled, he gave a little push and was off like a shot down the other side of the mountain, while we turned around and headed slowly back to camp. It would have been suicide for us to try to go down that steep incline with our dogs.

There was one trader up there who, for some reason, had won the enmity of a group of natives. One year he bought and paid for 4,000 pounds of whalebone, but when he arrived at Nome he had only 1,200 pounds. It was some time later that he was able to figure out what had happened. A group of natives, wanting to get even with him for some misdeed, had brought the bone aboard one side of his schooner and sold it to him. His ship was so small that he had no room in the hold for it so he piled it up on the other side of the deck. When he went to the hold to get merchandise to give them in exchange, the natives handed the whalebone back to accomplices who were in boats on the far side of the ship. They in turn brought it around to the other side of the ship and sold it all over again.

But these instances are rare in dealing with natives. Years after the incident of which I am telling in this chapter, we landed some supplies at Cape Saglasky for the Dalgostorg, the Soviet State Trading Organization. The goods were left on the beach and covered with tarpaulin. By chance, it was several months before they were taken away and some of the natives near by, who were experiencing a food shortage that year, appropriated some of the goods which they absolutely needed. But for everything they carted away they left furs in exchange which amply covered the value of the merchandise.

When I sailed for Seattle, following my first year as a full-fledged trader in Siberia, I went with the feeling that I had found the niche which I wanted to fill for the rest of my life. On board ship with me were two natives whom I liked and to whom I thought I would give a treat by showing them a little of what civilization was like. But when we got to port, both refused to leave the ship. The next day I came on board and finding them still there, I approached one of them, whom we called Jumbo.

"Jumbo, why don't you go ashore and look the city over?" I asked.

"Me no got compass," he said sadly.

I persuaded them to come ashore with me and took them for a ride in an automobile. They were terribly frightened and held on for dear life. When I seemed to miss another car by only a few inches, they grunted in their terror.

Back on the ship, the mate asked Jumbo what he thought of his ride.

"That sled he go like hell," Jumbo replied warmly. Plainly he was glad to have a solid deck under his feet again.

They were greatly mystified by the fact that "everybody turned his lights on at the same time." I couldn't understand what they meant for a long time, but after a great deal of explaining they finally made it clear. They were talking about the street lights.

When they got home the following spring, they naturally went in for a long program of telling their friends and relatives the facts about life in the great world outside. Of course they had a terrible time making anyone believe them. Jumbo's brother came to ask me scornfully whether it was true that there were talking ducks in Seattle. Thinking rapidly, I remembered that we had shown Jumbo a parrot and that there is a species of duck in Siberia which has a head very like that of a parrot, so I told the brother it was quite true.

CHAPTER VIII

UNTIL 1911, I spent alternate winters in and around Anadir. But while I loved the life, it caused a constant conflict in me, for it meant living abnormally, without any real home of my own. My wife, with our child, was in Seattle, and she worried much of the time about my living like an animal—or a Chuckcho, which is about the same thing.

And so, when, in 1911, my father met me in Seattle and proposed that we try ranching together, I decided to give up Siberia and trading, and live like a human being again. We located on some land in the Flathead Indian Reservation in Montana and undertook to raise cattle. I liked the country, I liked being at home again, and I liked the freedom of the range; but steers were slow, tedious beasts after polar bear and walrus, and the solid earth seemed too solid to be interesting, after the deck of a trading ship and the exciting insecurity of ice floes. Hence, my decision didn't stick a year. Leaving the ranch in care of some men who were better suited to the life than I was, I made a trip to Nome, Alaska, where I chartered a small schooner and did a spot of trading along the Russian coast, returning to the ranch in the fall.

In the spring of 1912, the Hibbard-Stewart Company, of Seattle, dealers in wool, hides, and furs, invited me to join them in a trading venture with Captain L. L. Lane under the name of Hibbard, Swenson and Lane. I accepted their proposal and we chartered the motor ship *Polar Bear* and made a successful trip along the Siberian coast that summer.

That was the year my father died. I immediately liquidated the ranch and returned to Seattle. In the spring of 1913, the Hibbards were engaged in negotiations with Captain Stephen Cottle for the purchase of his whaling ship, the *Belvedere,* and they again urged me to join them. We formed the Hibbard Swenson Company (a partnership which lasted until 1921) and bought the *Belvedere,* retaining Captain Cottle in command.

The years which I spent in partnership with the Hibbards were perhaps the most pleasant of my business life. From the time the company was formed until it was dissolved, in 1921, we never once had to look at our partnership agreement to settle any argument as to our relationship, for there were no arguments to settle. We expanded our business rapidly until we had several ships plying up and down the Arctic coasts, and our collections of furs were eagerly sought after because of their high quality. I would spend practically the entire winter season purchasing and assembling our trade cargo for the following season, making trips to the eastern markets and arranging factory shipments, supervising the packaging of goods so they would be of proper quality, the right size, and well wrapped. By the end of March or the first of April we would be loaded and ready to sail. Then we would leave for the Siberian coast to pick up our furs, finishing up about the middle of August.

Between seasons, we hunted walrus for their hides, oil, and ivory, calling at Point Barrow on the Alaskan side, and making two or three stops on the Siberian side to drop odds and ends of left-over cargo. This brought us back to Seattle about November first to begin the winter job. Sometimes we spent a part of the fall catching bowhead whales near Wrangel Island.

In addition to the actual trading which was done during the voyage, we bought large quantities of furs and ivory for cash. The ivory was largely walrus tusks, but there was always a considerable supply of mastodon and mammoth ivory, too, which originated in the north central part of Siberia, from the vicinity of the Indigirki and Lena rivers and as far west as the Province of Tobolsk.

This fossil ivory crop is one of the most amazing phenomena of the north. Mastodons and mammoths must have roamed the plains of Siberia in great numbers for the glaciers are still pouring forth mastodon remains in sufficient quantities to make tusks of definite commercial interest. The natives, of course, do not know that the tusks which they carefully gather and save to sell to the traders have come from an animal which was extinct long before recorded history began, and they explain the presence of the ivory by a theory that it comes from an animal which lives in the bowels of the earth which emerges to the surface to die. After its death the remains are spewed forth by the glaciers.

Those were good years, from 1912 to 1921, filled with variety and excitement. The northland was like a huge plantation to us, divided up into many fields, each of which produced a different crop. Along the coast of the Sea of Okhotsk we obtained ermine and great quantities of squirrel. In Kamchatka we found the finest red foxes (cherry red) in the world, and also the collections of Russian sable for which our company became famous. Farther north we collected quantities of white foxes, cross foxes, wolves, wolverine, deerskins, brown and polar bear skins, ivory, whalebone, and hair seal.

And they were good years from a business point of view, too, for the most part, though we did not become wealthy. If the market dropped on one article we would catch a rise on another, except at times when the bottom dropped out of everything, as it did in 1914 at the beginning of World War I. We never had what you would call an "average year." Seasons seemed to run in cycles, with one big year in four, just as every fourth year produces a tremendous run of salmon and a big catch of white foxes. Some of the Arctic skippers even believe in extreme ice every fourth year.

But those years were not without their misfortunes, man-made and otherwise. Of the latter, the most memorable was an earthquake at Ust Kamchatka, at the mouth of the Kamchatka River, which cost the lives of our Russian agent and his wife, as well as a financial loss amounting to more than $150,000. The visible effect of the earthquake, which occurred in the early spring of 1923, can best be described as a tidal wave of icebergs. It came that spring day without warning, before the ice in the bay had broken up; there was a mighty upsurge of water that rose to towering heights and, bearing on its crest the mountainous blocks of ice it had broken up in its rise, it advanced upon the land, annihilating everything in sight. In the space of a few moments it crushed and swept away two canneries that were in its path, as well as our supply warehouses and station, grinding to smithereens all of our equipment. The terrific crush of ice and water made a clean sweep of the beach, and the pressure of the millions of tons of ice carried everything inland before it for a distance of one mile. The body of the agent's wife was found three-quarters of a mile up the river, clad only in a nightgown. Twenty-seven people lost their lives.

The Kamchatka peninsula is on the same stratum of the earth's crust as the string of Japanese Islands, and it was later in the same year that the great earthquake occurred at Yokohama with such disastrous results. Kamchatka is a volcanic formation, and a number of its beautiful peaks are always spouting flame and smoke. One of these rocky capes near Ust Kamchatka, hurled into the sea by an eruption, probably caused the tidal wave.

Other unexpected things, too, happened to us from time to time. Just about the time we saw a tremendous profit ahead we would have a fire at sea, a shipwreck, a vessel icebound, or there would be a drop in the market, and the prospective huge profits would all be eaten up.

But even at times like that there was usually some additional excitement in store which would make life interesting.

In 1914, for instance, when the bottom dropped out of the fur market, we had a huge stock of furs on hand. We had thousands of white fox skins alone which we had bought at fourteen dollars apiece and which we had to sell for five dollars. We took such a serious licking that year that we might have gone out of business had not the American government wanted us to carry on.

We were whaling and hunting walrus, as well as trading,

and the government wanted all of the whale and walrus oil we could give them, because they were using these oils in the manufacture of explosives. The government also used our boats to transport coal and other supplies to the Pribilof Islands, thereby releasing some ships for other services.

It was during these years that I almost lost my life by drowning in the icy waters which break on the west shore of Kamchatka. It was a beautiful spring day, the first of May, the day of May baskets and rejoicing in our country because the cold winter has gone at last, and wild flowers are blooming in the woods, and the warmth of the sun has come back to earth again. But, although on that Siberian coast it was a beautiful day, too, the sun had done nothing to temper the water which surrounded us.

We had left ship in a launch and had taken with us a small sealing boat, for we knew that we would not be able to beach the launch in the heavy surf which was running. The chief engineer, a young Scotchman named George, two Portuguese sailors, and myself, started out. The Scotchman had no particular purpose in going ashore. He had joined us at the last minute, simply for entertainment, and it didn't occur to me to tell him that he had better stay aboard the launch, for no one would have thought anything disastrous or unpleasant could happen on such a beautiful day.

We landed safely and spent about an hour ashore, drinking tea and talking. When we got back to the sealing boat, accompanied by a Russian who wanted to go aboard, we found that while the tide had fallen somewhat, the sea had risen, so that the breakers were worse than ever. I noticed one which was unusually large and vicious, some distance from shore. They were breaking about every fifteen minutes and I hoped, as we got into the boat, that we would cross that spot at the right time.

Anton, one of our Portuguese sailors, was steering the boat, and I was pulling the bow oar, with the chief engineer, George, and the sailor at the others. Anton was a fine boatman in a whale-boat in the open sea, but apparently he had not had much experience handling a small boat in the surf. Or he may have become confused before we actually hit the big breaker. The proper method of getting through a spot like that is to hold the boat back when the breaker hits you, letting it slide back with the force of the water, until the impulse of the wave has passed, and then pull hard and fast to get through before another one comes along. We were away from the beach and well through the surf when Anton yelled, "Pull!" We pulled with all our might since there was nothing else to do, and it was no time to question his judgment. Anton had seen the blind-breaker ahead and he thought that by pulling hard, we could beat it, or get around the end of it, as it broke for only a distance of a hundred yards. The breaker hit us at an angle and over we went into water which was pouring in from a glacier-fed river. It was literally ice water. George, in a complete panic, cried out that he couldn't swim and I swam over to him and got him to hang on to the boat. Although we all tried to right the boat, it was impossible. As soon as we'd get it right side up, filled with water as it was, and one of the men would try to climb in, it would turn over like a barrel.

I decided that the longer we stayed there in that marrow-freezing water trying to right the boat, the more we diminished our chances of ever getting out alive, for I knew that no man could stand that temperature for long. I suggested that we swim to the launch, which was two or three hundred yards away, and I started out. But the longer I swam the farther away I seemed to be from the launch. Then I saw what was happening. The strong tide was carrying me parallel to the shore and I was making no headway at all.

Looking back, I saw that three of the others had started swimming for shore, and that George and the Russian were hanging onto the upturned boat. It was only about an eighth of a mile to shore, I think, but against that tide, and in water which was practically freezing, it seemed an endless distance. I have always been a fast and strong swimmer, but gradually my hands and arms got numb. My fingers felt as though they were a foot long and as thick as my arm. I was so impressed by this feeling that I held one of my hands up out of the water to convince myself that it was still normal. Then I began to swim harder than I ever had in my life before, for I was beginning to get little cramps in my arms and stomach from the icy water, and I knew that if I did not get to shore quickly, it would be too late.

When I was a little over halfway to shore, I noticed that the chief engineer was just behind me. He, too, had drifted down with the tide. Two oars from the boat drifted near us and he took one while I took the other. He stopped to rest with his oar under his arm. I put mine under my arm, too, but I kept on swimming as hard as I could.

And then I was in the midst of a huge breaker, the foam of which was seething over my head, so I let go of the oar.

It's strange what details you can remember at a time like this. As the breaker hit me, my cap went off and I thought with horror of the fact that the day before I had decided to go Russian and had had my head shaved. When the water hit my bare scalp I thought that my brains would be dashed out of my head. But I did have presence of mind enough to hold my nose and keep my mouth shut as the breaker enveloped me, for I knew that if that icy water got inside my stomach, I would be finished.

I have one other memory of that hell in the icy water. When my feet finally touched bottom near the beach I found that I couldn't stand up, and I had to go on swimming in water that was no more than four feet deep. Over my shoulder I could see big Anton, who was over six feet tall and a strong swimmer, standing up to his armpits in water, about to walk out. Then he turned his back to the land and yelled something in Portuguese to the other sailor, who was his cousin, and who was swimming close behind him. At that moment for some reason I will never know, the cousin started to swim back to the boat and Anton again plunged into the icy water and followed him.

When I finally got to a point where my knees touched sand, I found that there was a terrible undertow which was pulling me out to sea again, and it took the last ounce of strength I had to crawl up on the beach on all fours. The Russian whom we had come to visit was running toward me along the beach. I managed to stagger momentarily to my feet and wave at him. Then, without any conscious reason for doing so, I took my watch out of my pocket, broke the chain, and threw it away.

The Russian pulled off my boots and the heavy woolen shirt I was wearing, and put a sheepskin coat on me. Then he put my arm around his shoulders to support me, and walked me, half-conscious, up to the shack, about a quarter of a mile away. As soon as we got inside he undressed me and put me into a sleeping bag, but I had already lost consciousness.

When I came to I saw the chief engineer standing beside me. He looked at me and said, "Now who doesn't believe in Providence?" I asked him where the other boys were and he said that they were down on the beach, but that was a lie to spare me. The others were all drowned.

The next day we had to walk twenty-one miles down the coast to reach the spot where our ship was anchored. My legs and feet were terribly swollen and for a long time my whole body was so sore that I could neither sit nor stand comfortably. It took me two years to get over the mental effects of that ducking. I was just plain scared whenever we hit surf.

But it didn't make me want to leave the Arctic or the sea.

CHAPTER IX

In the spring of 1913, we outfitted the newly purchased *S.S. Belvedere*, at Seattle, having taken its master, Captain Stephen Cottle, along with the ship, for one of our regular trading trips to Siberia. Contrary to one of the superstitions of the sea, Captain Cottle had his wife with him. Everyone on board liked her. She was what, in any language, would be called a lovely lady. But the traditions of the sea are strong, and there was a good deal of silent objection to having a woman on board. I don't mean to say that there was any real enmity in the feeling or that it ever reached any serious proportions. It was only that as much as everyone liked and admired Captain Cottle, and his wife, too, for that matter, they would rather not have had her along.

I suppose that this feeling about having a woman aboard an Arctic ship arises less from superstition (common to all sailors) than from practical considerations. The hazards of Arctic seamanship are comparatively great and include the constant danger of running into long periods of isolation and complete loss of contact with civilization. If the food runs short, or if members of the crew become sick, it's something that men take for granted once they have entered the Arctic. But if there is a woman on board, and she becomes ill or has to suffer privation along with the men, there is an inevitable and automatic feeling of chivalry which makes it seem a necessity to put in at some port, at the loss of a lot of valuable time. In the case of whalers, this also means loss of money to the crew, since most of them are paid on the basis of the season's catch.

However, we felt fortunate in having Cottle.in command of the ship for he was an excellent navigator in ice. He was a whaler with many years' experience behind him, and he knew how to take advantage of the ice so that it became an asset instead of a liability.

Handling a ship in ice is very different from taking care of it in open water. If it is necessary to lay up, you do not anchor, but instead, tie up to the ice. Anchored securely, a ship may easily be crushed by the movement of the ice packs, but if you run a cable along the ice and tie to a hummock, the ship will follow with the shifting of the ice. At other times it is necessary to find a suitable place behind heavy cakes or grounded ridges, so that if the ice starts jamming, the ship will be protected. A fresh water supply must also be taken into consideration. A good captain of a ship in the ice will find a supply of fresh water near which to tie up, as surely as a leader of a regiment will find a water supply for his men on the march. In glacier ice the water will melt at the top and find its way into a depression or hollow in the mass and accumulate there as though it were a tank or cistern. Since melting ice to provide water for a large crew is a terrific job, even if the supply of fresh glacier ice is plentiful, it is easy to see the advantage of locating a cistern of fresh water.

In addition to the tremendously detailed knowledge of general ice navigation, familiarity with local conditions is also absolutely essential. Along the Alaskan Arctic coast to the eastward you have to stay close in shore in order to avoid, as far as possible, the risk of being jammed by the ice, and this is likewise true along the Siberian shore to the westward. The ice grounds in shallow water have tremendous pressure behind them, but if you can get your ship in behind that mass of jammed, grounded ice on the leeward side of it, as it were (away from the drift), it forms a perfect barrier and the ship will be safe as long as the ice holds.

Captain Cottle knew all of these factors, just as a good cook knows how much salt to put in chicken gravy; we felt secure with the ship in his hands, and were not inclined to grumble about the violation of tradition caused by his wife's presence.

Meanwhile, Vilhjalmur Stefansson had equipped the *Karluk* and two small schooners and had sailed from Vancouver, B.C., on his third Arctic expedition under the auspices of the Canadian Government, in an attempt to add to the important knowledge he had already contributed on the life of the Eskimos, and other scientific data. This expedition was undertaken to enable him to investigate his theory that it was possible to sustain human life even in parts of the Arctic where no man had ever lived. He believed that he could go into regions which even the Eskimos had not penetrated because they believed these regions could not sustain life, and that he could travel indefinitely, carrying on scientific or other work, depending entirely on the resources of the country for food and fuel. Both of the elements necessary to human life he expected to get from animals—food from the flesh and fuel from their fat. The story of the expedition, of what he learned, and of the catastrophe which fell upon him, he himself has told in *The Friendly Arctic.* I do not wish to repeat his story but only to tell that part of it which touched upon my own life and that of the crew of the *Belvedere.*

After leaving the Siberian coast on our first trip on the *Belvedere,* we called at Nome, Alaska, to pick up freight for the Stefansson expedition and for the Mounted Police stationed at Herschel Island, about seventy-five miles from Demarcation Point, the boundary between Alaska and Canada along the Arctic shore. As we pushed away from Nome for Herschel Island, in the middle of August (a time when Los Angeles and New York were doubtless sweltering with heat), we encountered some of the worst ice conditions which had afflicted the Arctic for years. Soon we were caught fast, unable to move either onward to Herschel Island or back to port at Nome. As always happens at a time like this, we were not without company. Nearby was the *Polar Bear* captained by L. L. Lane, with whom the Hibbard-Stewart Company and I had been associated in a trade venture in 1912. Not far away was the motorship *Elvira* under the command of Captain C. T. Pedersen, a veteran Arctic skipper; and also one of Stefansson's small schooners. All were as incapable of movement as we.

Indeed, the *Elvira* had been so badly damaged by the ice that Pedersen abandoned her, and brought his entire crew onto the *Belvedere* where we received them as guests for the long winter.

No one knew the whereabouts of the *Karluk,* the main ship of the Stefansson expedition. She was commanded by Captain Bob Bartlett and Stefansson had left Nome aboard her. News travels fast, however, by the "tundra wireless," the mouth-to-mouth passage of information from native village to native village, which manages to keep everyone in the Arctic fairly well informed of what is going on. There was a unanimity of opinion that she had been caught in the ice and was drifting to the westward, for it was known that while the *Mary Sachs* of the Stefansson expedition, commanded by Captain Peter Bernard (who had a great deal of local ice experience) had kept close to shore, Captain Bartlett had taken the *Karluk* on an offshore lead, and no one saw how she could have escaped becoming fast in the ice and drifting towards the Siberian Arctic.

I was extremely anxious to get news of our position to the Mounted Police on Herschel Island, about sixty-five miles away, and let them know that we had aboard their supplies and the Stefansson supplies, which were to have been delivered at the same place.

Consequently, about the middle of September, Arnold Castle and Dan Sweeney (sailors), Thompson, a native from Indian Point, and myself, started on the sixty-five mile trip across the ice with a small Yukon sled, a tent, a small stove built from two kerosene cans, and a few supplies. We felt sure that we could make it in three days, or four at the outside.

About fifteen miles from the ship we struck open water along the beach caused by an outlet from a lagoon. In order to get to the other side we were forced to take to the sea ice and make a detour of several miles off shore.

Thompson, the native, didn't like the looks of it and shook his head in disapproval.

"Now summer time, no winter yet," he objected, but we kept on.

We kept the sled in the middle, with a line out from each corner, spread apart as much as possible to keep the weight widely distributed, and even kept our feet wide apart in the same effort. Sweeney, who was the lightest man in the outfit, went ahead, Castle and I followed on ropes opposite each other, and "Summer Time" Thompson brought up the rear.

Sweeney had no difficulty skimming over the ice, even though at every step it gave like a rubber blanket. But suddenly I, being much heavier, felt myself slipping. I let out a yell to "hold everything!" and then found myself in water up to my armpits. The only reason I wasn't in over my head was that I had instinctively thrown out my arms as I went down and they had checked my course when they hit the ice.

There I lay, my arms out over the ice like the front flippers of a walrus, vainly trying to climb up, only to have the ice break through every time I put my weight on it. Castle also had started to go through, but had thrown himself on the sled, and although that eventually went down, too, he managed to slide off it and regain his feet on solid ice.

While Sweeney and Castle were running around in circles trying to find something—a pole, a rope, a ladder— (almost anything of that kind which might be lying around on top a frozen ocean!) to extend to me, and, of course, could find nothing, I kept plowing a furrow through the ice in my efforts to get to the top. Finally, good old Thompson, the accurate weather man, who had doubtless seen more than one of his native friends in exactly my predicament, went at the job systematically. Lying on his belly, he wriggled slowly toward me until I could reach his extended hands. Then he put his entire mechanism in reverse and I slid slowly out onto the ice like a seal.

The miracle of it was that, having saved my life, he never reproached me with a word or a look for having made it necessary, by my obstinate disregard of his good advice, to do so.

After I was on my feet I was heavier than ever, for my clothing was soaked with water, and I had to use the motions of a man on skates to keep from breaking through again. For fully an hour we maneuvered to get the sled out safely without all of us going in, I, of course, working in my soaked clothing. By the time we finally got the pick under one runner and slid the sled to comparative safety again, I would have traded my beloved Arctic for almost any spot south of the Mason and Dixon line.

None of us carried any extra change of clothes and after a night of drying out in a tent on shore before our tin can stove, I fighting to keep bare knees from roasting and bare back from freezing, we found the ice frozen solidly enough to proceed without further immersions. However, we did not reach Herschel Island in four days. It took two weeks. Meanwhile, we had run out of food. But as luck would have it, we fell in with a group of natives also bound for Herschel, and they killed several seals and sea-gulls. We didn't eat any of the sea-gulls, but the seal liver was delicious.

When we got in sight of the island we found open water between us and land. We finally emulated George Washington crossing the Delaware and made shore by mounting a cake of ice and paddling in.

Later, when we had made our way back to the *Belvedere,* we found that we would have to do something to replenish her food supplies. We had brought with us enough of everything for our own use, but with Captain Pedersen's men on board minus supplies of their own, our consumption had doubled.

The men were a good lot and took it well. But they relieved themselves of their feelings from time to time about this misfortune and the fact that Captain Cottle's wife was on board, led to a rather innocent game of baiting.

The captain and his wife had a cabin adjoining the dining salon, ventilated by lattice work just under the ceiling, so that when anyone was talking in the dining room Mrs. Cottle in her cabin could overhear everything that was being said.

The captain had given strict orders rationing the eggs, of which we were especially short. Each man, I believe, was to receive one strip of bacon and an egg once a week. The captain and his wife were included in the rationing and she, as it happened, was very fond of eggs.

Needless to say, the men accepted the rationing with complete good humor and were fully co-operative about it. But they knew Mrs. Cottle's fondness for eggs, and as I have said, feeling a certain resentment about her presence on board (which now, almost more than when we had been under way, was hindering them in their natural inclination to swear and talk and act as they pleased), they delighted in making her think that they were getting all the eggs they wanted while she was getting none. We would sit down to breakfast and the chief engineer would say in a voice loud enough so that he was sure she could hear it: "Pass the ham and eggs." A moment later someone would speak up and say: "Gee, these eggs taste swell." This went on morning after morning, without an egg anywhere in sight. Poor Mrs. Cottle never said anything to us about it, but every few days she would go into the galley and approach the steward.

"Did you serve eggs for breakfast this morning?" she would ask anxiously.

"No, ma'am," he would say shortly.

Then her face would cloud with exasperation and she would stamp her foot.

"I know you served eggs," she would say. "I heard them talking about it. I know they were eating eggs."

It wasn't exactly what you would call chivalrous, but it was, after all, a pretty harmless way for the men to relieve their feelings in a tremendously difficult situation.

Supplies had to be secured somehow, and since Captain Pedersen and I were both restless at the thought of spending the entire winter aboard ship, we decided we would strike out overland by dog sled to Fairbanks, Alaska. Several others on board decided to go along, also. Captain Lane of the *Polar Bear* wanted to get out, too, but Lane and his party thought that it would be best to go by way of Fort McPherson, while Pedersen and I decided to strike out directly overland from where the ship lay, thus saving four or five hundred miles, even though the route we would take was one which had never before been successfully traveled by white men. The seven-hundred-mile trip which the short route represented was far enough in any case. We did not want to add four or five hundred miles to it.

Everyone to whom we talked tried to persuade us not to go by that route. We were urged to make the trip either through Fort McPherson, or by way of Rampart House on the Porcupine River, and down the river from there, which was the trail that most travelers took. But whether because we wanted to be the first white men to take the hard way, or simply because we wanted to save distance, Pedersen and I decided definitely to take the short cut and let Lane go any way he chose. However, we wanted to co-operate with Lane in equipping the two parties and so we tried to get dogs for both of us. Pedersen's idea, and mine, was that we would round up and buy as many dogs as possible (and it was no easy task to get anywhere near the number we needed) and then divide them up between the two parties, equally in both number and quality. Captain Lane, however, did not co-operate in this plan and so we followed the principle of each party for itself.

While we were getting our dogs together and preparing for the trip, I bought a large catch of over three hundred white fox skins from a trapper named Ole Andreasen, and decided to take them with us overland on our sled. The skins were left in a camp with an Eskimo, whose "fox skin name" was Enuk. In giving you his name, he would always say, "My fox skin name is Enuk, but my real name is Arshugrer," the formula which most of the natives used who had been baptized by missionaries. This arose from the missionaries' custom of exacting tribute for baptism. A missionary baptized a native and gave him a Christian name, receiving a fox skin in exchange. We had arranged to take Enuk and his wife with us on our trip because they could furnish us with two dog teams which we needed badly. We found both Enuk and his wife in high spirits. Enuk had a new .22 rifle, a couple of cans of fruit and other supplies, and Mary, his wife, stood grinning at us, and dangling a new piece of cheap jewelry from her hand. I asked Enuk how this good fortune had come to them and he told me that Captain Lane had been the donor. Then the story came out.

It really went back to the days when Lane and I had been in business together. He had always enjoyed a practical joke, so long as it was on someone else, but he had never grown up to the point where he could have his fun even if he didn't come out ahead. Now with both of us planning the difficult and hazardous trip across country to Fairbanks, he had a tremendous desire to beat Pedersen and me and get there first, even though it had not officially been declared a race to be run completely according to rule. His desire was heightened by the fact that Nome had received definite information that the Stefansson expedition had been lost, and in the mail which Pedersen and I would carry out there were letters and telegrams carrying news of the misadventure. Somehow or other, Lane could not resist the temptation to get to Fairbanks first, so that he could bear to the outside world the news of the lost expedition. Therefore, knowing that we had planned to take Enuk and his wife with us, he had gone to see them and, showering them with presents, had instructed them to go ahead until we got over the divide, that is, over the worst of the traveling. Then they were to stop our progress by having Mary play sick, so that we should have to lay up there. Meanwhile, Lane was planning to follow in the trail which we had broken until he caught up with us, leave us behind to allow Mary to recuperate, and he would get to Fort Yukon before we could, to broadcast the news to the world.

That information only caused us all to re-double our efforts. We set out as soon as possible and went into the interior. Every day we would start traveling at five in the morning and keep on all day until we could travel no farther at night because of exhaustion. We took the finest possible care of our dogs to save their strength. Even Pedersen and I wore harnesses and pulled with the dogs. If we saw them failing a little, we would stop to give them a rest. Let one of them show the slightest evidence of sore feet, and we put boots on him. At night we bedded them down in brush, sometimes giving them better beds than we had for ourselves.

Then we began to play with Captain Lane, who, we were quite sure, was coming close behind us. We managed to leave little messages for him. At one place we crossed a stream where there was an open spot of water so clear that we could see trout swimming around. Here we wrote a note to him on the heavy frost on the ice, saying, "Good fishing here," and misdated it, so that when Lane's party found it, they would think that they were rapidly overtaking us.

Pedersen took charge of cutting wood for the fires and getting the camps ready, while I took care of the dogs, pampering them as though they were babies. I always liked dogs and had had a lot of experience with them, and on this trip they were so important to us that they came in for the same treatment as the human members of the expedition.

There was no difference in their food and ours. We had a big pot along. In it we would boil some rice and whatever game we had picked up that day, usually some ptarmigan or rabbit, and stew the whole mess together. After taking a couple of scoops out of the pot for ourselves the dogs got the rest.

Five days from the coast we got into a terrific snowstorm, which completely obscured the sky, and made the entire world about us one whirling mass of white, with nothing to give any indication of direction. We had a small compass with us and Pedersen took it out, so that we could follow our direction by that. But in looking at it, he dropped it into the fine snow at our feet. We both went down on our hands and knees to look for it, but without success. Then we began to pan the snow, taking it up a scoopful at a time to examine every particle. We kept at it for some time but we never did find that compass. At last we gave up and from there on we followed the natural trend of the watershed, which got us into some tremendous detours, and without doubt took us far off from the shortest way.

Following this route, we hit Lake Chandler, which we had not expected to come upon. Here we went to the house of an Indian named Peter. We were short of dog feed and we needed more dogs, both of which Peter had. All in all, we decided that it would be advantageous to add him to the outfit. We asked him how far it was to Fort Yukon and

Driving dogs, Kamchatka

he said, "Twenty-six sleeps." That seemed absolutely impossible to us, and we told him so. Finally, he grudgingly consented to estimate that perhaps it was no more than "twenty sleeps." He knew that we wanted him to go with us and he was trying to hold out for as high a price as possible. We also realized that he was trying to hold us up, yet, with some of his dogs and with his knowledge of short cuts, we knew that we could make better time with him, and we were still trying desperately to beat Lane. Eventually, we bribed him with a watch, and the promise of ten dollars a day, and started out over an old Hudson's Bay trail.

Captain Pedersen was a great fellow to get up early in the morning and I could always count on him routing me out by five; but Peter liked to sleep and when wakened would always grumble and turn over again. Unfortunately he had a watch and could tell time, so that it did no good to tell him it was seven or eight o'clock in the morning, when, by looking at his watch he could see that it was really only five; but Pedersen took care of this. Before waking Peter in the morning, he would stealthily get the fellow's watch and turn it ahead a couple of hours. Then sometime during the day he would manage to get it again and turn it back, in order to keep Peter from complaining that we were traveling too late. At times we ran into such light, deep snow that we had to double-track with snow-shoes before we got the dogs through with their loads.

Four days away from Peter's camp we ran short of dog feed again. But apparently Providence was looking out for us; we suddenly stumbled onto a deserted cabin, where we found a lot of dried moose meat hanging and a quarter of a pound of green tea. Of course, we took it, but we arranged with Peter to replace its equivalent on his return trip.

Somehow, in dividing the meat, Peter felt that he did not get his share and blamed Enuk for it. From then on until we got to Fort Yukon and Peter started back, the two natives never spoke to each other. Up to this time, when we camped at night (we carried no tents and slept in the open), we had always made one big fire and had all sat around it, a united group. But after Peter and Enuk quarreled, we had three fires. The large fire in the center was used by all of us except the two natives; each of them had a little fire of his own at opposite sides of the group. And where before we had all slept in a group, with our feet as near the fire as possible, now Peter and Enuk each slept by his individual fire, with the group separating them.

Enuk was rather temperamental about his food, too. The natives in the North do not like green tea. They want black tea, because they seem to like the color of it, as well as the taste; but we had run out of black tea and had only the green which we had found with the moose meat. When we brewed it that first night Enuk looked at the pale result with complete disgust.

"More better put some coffee in it," he said.

"No," I said to him. "We have only enough coffee for one meal as it is. If you are going to make tea, make tea."

But Enuk only grunted at me as I turned away. And when later he brought me a cup of tea, it had the foulest, brownish-black color I had ever seen, and an even fouler taste. Regardless of my orders, he had put the coffee in it.

Peter, meanwhile, furnished considerable comic relief.

He had only a few words of English and he loved to use them. We would be going along, with no sign of human habitation visible, when suddenly Peter would say, "Bom bye, I got house." A few minutes later, sure enough, we would come to some sort of a house, completely deserted and perhaps practically fallen to pieces, but nevertheless a house. Then for hours we would continue in silence until Peter, suddenly becoming articulate again, would say, "Bom bye, I got another house." And sure enough, in a few minutes we would pass another building of some sort.

I began to think that he was more prosperous than his camp would indicate, when suddenly I heard him say, "Bom bye, I got river." And a little later, "Bom bye, I got lake." Then I realized what he was trying to say was that soon we would come to a house, or a river, or a lake.

On the whole, the trip was one of the most pleasant I have ever made. We were surrounded constantly by the beauty of snow and ice and frost. In some places in the interior there is absolutely no wind and the air is extremely dry. The frost forms on the ice and trees in great, thick incrustations. If you bump one of the trees, it comes down in a tremendous shower of crystals, clear and sparkling. Pedersen was such a good traveling companion, and Enuk and Peter, on the whole, such good fun, that all in all, we had a grand time.

I never shall forget the last day of our trip going into Fairbanks. We made fifty-three miles that day and that had meant fifty-three miles of walking and running. We did not have enough dogs to permit us to add our weight to their loads. That morning we had made up our minds to finish the trip by night, and Pedersen and I took turns breaking trail. There were mile-posts on the government trail between Circle City and Fairbanks, fifty-three of them. First, Pedersen would run ahead of the dogs until he had counted eight of them and then I would run ahead until I had counted eight, too. It was snowing, and there was a terrific gale; everybody at Circle City had cautioned us against trying to go through the pass, warning us that we would never get over the mountain; but Pedersen and I were both determined that Lane was not going to make monkeys of us. We had a hunch that once over the mountain we would find better weather, so we put ropes around our waists, tied the other ends to the lead dogs and actually dragged them up the mountain and through the pass. Just as we had expected, we found better weather on the other side and the rest of the going was simple. We got into Fairbanks at eleven o'clock that night, having started the last fifty-three-mile stretch at five that morning. The whole trip had taken us twenty-six days, a record for speed in that country.

We went to the hotel at Fairbanks, and you may imagine what even the comparative comforts of a Fairbanks hotel looked like after the twenty-six days and nights through which we had just passed. We had stood the trip very well, as a matter of fact, and there was really nothing to complain of, but just the same, we were drooping with fatigue, and a wash and a bed seemed just about the two most beautiful things in the world.

I don't believe either Pedersen or I gave a moment's consideration to the fact that our native fur clothing was torn and worn and dirty. We were feeling rather pleased with ourselves and not at all like the tough hombres we must have looked.

But the hotel clerk saw us from another point of view. He sized us up and put us both in a little room about eight by ten, with two rickety cots in it and no window. Well, all things are comparative, and here we were—in Paradise. It never occurred to either of us to make a fuss. We gladly went at the business of digging in for the night.

But we hadn't gone very far with our preparations when some newspaper men, who knew what it was all about from the mail and telegrams we had disposed of before checking in at the hotel, rushed in to interview us. We told them all we knew and then one of them looked around the room and laughed.

"Did you fellows ask for a room like this?" he said.

I looked up in surprise, realizing for the first time what kind of a hole we had been given, and told him that we had not thought anything about it. He went downstairs and in a few minutes the clerk came up and, of course, moved us to the finest room in the hotel.

Ten days later Captain Lane reached Fairbanks, and one of the greatest pleasures we have ever had was seeing the look on his face when he found us there. It was worth all the effort we had made.

CHAPTER X

WHEN I reached Seattle I learned more about the Stefansson expedition than I had been able to find out at Nome. The *Karluk,* steaming to the north, had been caught in the ice and, because they had been short of fresh meat, Stefansson, Burt McConnell and Wilkins had left the ship to go ashore and get some caribou. During their stay ashore the ice pack broke loose before the wind and drifted to the westward, taking the *Karluk* with it.

But much as I regretted the possibility that so gallant an explorer as Stefansson had perished and that perhaps his crew were in desperate need of rescue, my principal job was to take care of my own people on the *Belvedere,* which I had left frozen fast in the ice at Icy Reef near Demarcation Point. For, with Captain Pedersen's crew from the *Elvira* also aboard, they would be embarrassingly short of supplies by spring.

And so, when we outfitted the *King and Winge* in Seattle and started north with her the following spring, it was principally to take supplies to the *Belvedere* and to continue with our usual trading trip later. We met her, replenished her, and made our regular trip along the Siberian coast, then called at Nome. Here, for the first time, I met Burt McConnell.

Meanwhile, Captain Pedersen had replaced the *Elvira* with the *Herman* and at Emma Harbor, Siberia, he had picked up Captain Bob Bartlett, commander of the *Karluk,* who brought news that his boat had been crushed by the ice near Wrangel Island and sunk. Several of the expedition members had left in advance of Bartlett's main party, in an attempt to reach land quickly, and had been lost. The others, proceeding more cautiously with Bartlett, had eventually reached Wrangel Island and were in desperate straits. Bartlett, with one of the Eskimos in his party, had risked the dangers of crossing a hundred miles of hazardous ice to the Siberian mainland, in order to get news of the *Karluk's* plight to the world.

Bartlett had made the trip from the island to the mainland without mishap, a distance which is shown on the chart as 110 miles, but which is actually several hundred miles to a man walking around open water and hummocks, among the most hazardous ice conditions imaginable. It had taken him thirty days to make the trip—an average speed of three or four miles a day which, to my mind, is evidence of extraordinary skill in ice. He reached the Siberian coast at Cape North and, traveling along the coast, met a Russian official, Baron Kleist, who took him to Emma Harbor.

At Saint Michaels, Captain Bartlett had sent news of the plight of the *Karluk* crew to the government, and two United States revenue cutters, the *Bear* and the *Thetis*, had been detailed to try to get the men off the island. Meanwhile, the Russian government had also sent two ice-breakers—the *Taimyr* and the *Vaigatch*—which were to make the same attempt. But although these four boats had headed for Wrangel, none of them had actually been able to get through the closely packed ice. Captain Bartlett himself had accompanied the *Bear* on two trips, but unfavorable ice conditions had prevented their reaching the island.

When I met Burt McConnell, he urged me to make the attempt to take the men off in the *King and Winge,* and took me to see Captain Bartlett, who added his plea to that of McConnell's. Meanwhile, Captain L. L. Lane, against whom Pedersen and I had raced across Alaska, was again in northern waters, aboard the *Polar Bear.* It will be remembered that up to this time, even when news of the crew of the *Karluk* reached civilization, the general impression was that Stefansson and Wilkins (who had become separated from the party) had been lost on the ice. It is easy then to imagine Captain Lane's surprise when, cruising near Cape Kellett, he ran into Stefansson. Stefansson tells the story of Lane's "rescue" of him in *The Friendly Arctic.**

"When I got to the end of the sandspit, half a mile from the ship, a whaleboat was lowered and came towards land with six men rowing and three or four passengers. Through my binoculars I recognized Captain Lane, Constable Jack Parsons of the Herschel Island Mounted Police, and Herman Kilian, engineer of the *Polar Bear.* Presently I heard from the approaching boat shouts of 'He's not an Eskimo. He's got field glasses—he must be one of the crew of the *Sachs.*' Presently I heard Constable Parsons say, 'I think that's Stefansson,' to which Captain Lane replied, 'Don't you think it. The fishes ate him long ago.' A few yards nearer I heard Kilian say, 'By God, that is Stefansson.' There were contradictions from several others but my identification was soon agreed on and Captain Lane shouted an order: 'Don't a damn one of you move till I shake hands with him!' The boat touched the beach and the captain jumped out. His men delayed just long enough to obey

---

* Vilhjalmur Stefansson, *The Friendly Arctic*—Page 374-f.

him and then scrambled out after, and I received the most enthusiastic welcome of my whole life.

"Assuredly the idea most definitely connected with the Arctic seems to be one of starvation, and Captain Lane's first thought was what he could give me to eat. He said he had the best cook that ever came to the Arctic and that the ship was full of good things. Now what would I like? I had only to say what I wanted and the cook would prepare me the finest dinner I ever saw. I tried to make clear that while I was hungry for news my appetite for food was very slight. In fact, the excitement had taken away what little I might have had. As for that, I had been in the North so long that I could think of nothing so good as exactly what we had been eating on shore—caribou meat. I had the delicacy to refrain from stating to Captain Lane that none of his food was as good, but I tried to put him off by explaining how eager I was for all sorts of news that I knew he could tell me. But these diplomatic protests evidently rather worried him, so I finally asked for some canned corn. Corn has always been my favorite vegetable yet I don't think I had eaten half a dozen spoonfuls before I forgot to continue."

I finally consented to make the attempt to rescue Bartlett's crew and we started out on the *King and Winge*. Burt McConnell came along as a guest and companion and Captain Bartlett went back on the revenue cutter *Bear*. When you start out on a job like this in the Arctic, it does not cancel the attempts of anyone else, for no one knows whether he is going to get through or not, and every ship that attempts it takes chances of failure and disaster, so the *Bear* went right on with her efforts while we, in the *King and Winge*, went ahead with our expedition.

We headed first for East Cape because I wanted some

natives and some skin boats for the work that was ahead of us. The natives' boats, all made by hand according to the most primitive methods and using only the materials which their own region affords, are the product of generations of combat with the ice, and are the best boats for work at close quarters in the frozen seas of the North. They are light enough to be carried over the ice, yet strong and elastic enough to easily withstand pressure from the ice which would demolish a factory-made product of America. With one of these skin boats (or umiak), thirty-five natives, and some dogs, we headed for Wrangel Island. I knew that if we were blocked by the ice, as the *Bear* had been, we could, with any luck at all, reach the island with the umiak, which could be dragged over the ice by the natives, launched whenever we reached a patch of open water, pulled out again if we encountered another ice field, and the process repeated over and over again for a hundred miles if necessary.

Wrangel Island was about six hundred miles away. For the first four hundred we encountered very little ice. Then gradually ice-floes began to appear, and increased in number. Some were black with walrus, and the crew looked with longing eyes at the potentialities of such fine hunting, but we could not stop. Soon we were in ice in earnest and the plucky little *King and Winge* had to dodge and turn in every direction, backing up and starting over again as she plowed her way through. Sometimes, at full speed ahead, she would literally climb up on an ice-floe, her prow sliding over the edge like a polar bear's paws, until she had broken it down with her own weight. Fortunately, Captain

Jochimsen was a veteran in the ice and knew how to use every trick.

For eighty miles we fought the ice, at times passing ridges almost as tall as our masts; we never would have gotten through had it not been for the skill, the courage, and the persistence of Captain Jochimsen, together with the staunchness of the *King and Winge* herself.

As we came within sight of the sandy beach of Rodgers Harbor, where Captain Bartlett had told us we would find the men, we saw scant signs of human life. There was a small tent, a flag-pole and a cross visible, but we saw no men, no dogs and no sleds. We crowded the deck and waited in dreadful anticipation and with very little to say to each other, while the chief engineer blew long, repeated blasts on the whistle. For a long time there was no stir of life whatever. Finally, a man came slowly from the tent, looking confused and a little startled. He brushed his hand across his eyes as if he could scarcely believe what he saw. Then he turned slowly and going back into the tent, emerged in a moment with the British flag, which he raised to the top of the flag-pole. Two other men came out of the tent and stood staring at us without any signs of excitement or even welcome. They were simply stupefied.

We lowered a skin boat and started ashore with some natives. As the umiak approached, one of the men detached himself from the group and ran down to the beach with a rifle in his hand, pumping it madly; the natives, who had been paddling forward, suddenly began to reverse their course, apparently thinking that he was going to shoot half of them. They kept repeating that he was crazy, and they wanted to go back to the boat, but I calmed them and we went on. Later we found out that what he had been doing was emptying out all the shells, whether in sheer confusion or to assure us that he was unarmed, I didn't know. But in a sense, it had the same effect as a salute fired from a warship—to prove to an approaching vessel that the guns are empty.

Just what went through the natives' minds I did not know, but after they got on the beach they all quite solemnly began to turn somersaults. I never was able to get an explanation of why they did this, but I think they were motivated by some superstition, some feeling that they had to appease this mad, white God.

By now the other two men had come down to the beach and though all three of them were men with whom Burt McConnell had been closely associated on the *Karluk,* he could not recognize any of them. Their haggard, sunken eyes were almost concealed by shaggy mops of hair. Their faces were unlike those of any man I have ever seen in my life. They were filthy with dirt, emaciated, furrowed with wrinkles, and covered with sores and scabs. Their clothes, in which they had lived and slept for seven months, were in tatters, and their drawn, tense, bright eyes told more volubly than words the story of their sufferings and hopelessness.

For more than a month they had been living on white fox carcasses. Wrangel Island is a breeding place for white fox in the summer time, so there were always plenty of them. The men were not equipped with boats so could do very little seal hunting; they had been forced to fall back on the white fox, an animal whose flesh is the most terrible thing in the world to eat. The fat is terribly strong and all of the flesh is nauseating. The natives won't touch it and neither will the natives' dogs, even if they are half starving. Yet these men had had practically nothing else to eat for over a month.

When we had all calmed down enough to talk to each other, we discovered that the man who had greeted us with his rifle was James Munro, chief engineer of the *Karluk*, who had been left in command of the island when Bartlett made his ice trip to Siberia. The other two men were Templeman, the steward, and F. W. Maurer. Years later, Maurer, with two or three other men, went back to Wrangel Island in an attempt to prove Stefansson's theory that life could be sustained by the resources of the country; but whether their knowledge was insufficient, or whether the theory itself is impractical, they became ill with scurvy, and in attempting to reach the Siberian mainland across the ice, they all lost their lives.

We took the men back to the ship in the skin boat and with considerable difficulty got the *King and Winge* under way. The ice was moving before a southwest wind and there was danger of its closing in and blocking our attempt to return to open water, crushing the *King and Winge* as it had done in the past to many whaling ships in that vicinity, and so we lost no time. Again we fought our way through the eighty miles we had already covered with such difficulty, and just as we came out of the ice into open water, we found the revenue cutter *Bear* steaming back and forth, looking for an opening. They came down at us and Captain Bartlett came aboard, looked the men over and said, "Well, well, we'll take them aboard the revenue cutter." The men did not want to go. They wanted to stay with us on the *King and Winge*, but Bartlett was their boss and they had no choice but to be sent back home. We on the *King and Winge* went on about our business.

CHAPTER XI

I SUPPOSE most men who have followed the sea for a number of years accumulate a few superstitions. When an old sailor on a whaling ship tells you not to whistle while you are on the ship, it is best not to laugh at him. He means it. And I had my superstitions, too, chief among which was a fear of Friday, the thirteenth. But you may examine some of the evidence.

In 1910 I was preparing for a trip on which my wife wanted to go, bringing along our son, then six years old. I liked having her with me, but I had a premonition about taking her on this trip, and urged her not to go. Of course, she laughed at my fears and came along. We sailed on Friday, the thirteenth. A few days later diphtheria broke out on the ship. Our boy contracted it, and just after we arrived at Nome, Alaska, he died. I never have been able to forget the fact that the trip began on Friday, the thirteenth.

Eleven years later, about the first or second of April, 1921, I sailed from Seattle on the *M.S. Kamchatka,* on one of our regular trading expeditions. She was a fine strong ship and had previously been the old whaling ship named *The Thrasher,* after a killer whale. The frames had originally been built for a much larger vessel and had been used in this smaller ship to give it additional strength. She had what was considered the strongest nose in the whaling fleet, a heavy oak structure which could buck ice at full speed and plow through it. There was oak fore and aft and we had

127

her sheathed with three-inch Australian iron bark, the toughest wood in the world. There was a lot of pitch pine in her, too.

She had about her a wonderful odor of old sea days. For years she had been used in active whaling and was soaked with whale oil from timbers to skin. If you could have pressed out of her all the oil she had soaked up you probably could have lighted a house with whale oil lamps for a year. Then there was the smell of that fine pitch pine and old oak. Altogether, she smelled delicious!

There were twenty-three of us aboard all told, seasoned men, with a good skipper and chief, and a cargo made up of five tons of gunpowder in the forepeak, about a thousand cases of ammunition, and a whole deck load of drums of gasoline. In addition, there were about two hundred cases of distillate which had been delivered to us through an error of the oil company's. Since we didn't discover it until most of it was loaded, it seemed simpler to take it along and try to dispose of it than to unload it again. So we piled it on deck forward and let it go. In the forward deck-house we had our regular light trading supplies: woolen socks, heavy pants, shirts, mackinaws, guns, knives, food—we were practically a floating department store. Everything was as usual except for the highly inflammable, explosive cargo, which always makes a man feel a little uncomfortable at sea.

It was a calm, uneventful trip until about the tenth, when we ran into a terrific storm. Going across from Seattle to the Siberian coast, we were headed westward, pushing into heavy seas and headwinds all the time. Gradually the winds rose and suddenly we were in the middle of one of those snorters which you hit every now and then; one of those storms which act as though they were going to blow the top of the world off. We were making no progress at all. With full steam ahead we could only make steerage way, just keeping ourselves with our nose into it. We weren't getting anywhere at all, just plunging madly up the side of one mountain of water and sliding down the other side like hell on wheels, with half an ocean splashing over us at every plunge.

However, the *Kamchatka* was too good a ship to let us down. As bad as this storm was, we all knew that she had weathered worse ones, so we just kept our pumps going, kept her nose into it, and waited for the blow to end. But I didn't like it when the engineer reported that there was a lot of kerosene floating around in the bilge. The *Kamchatka* had Diesel engines and we had aboard quite a lot of coal oil in tanks, which we used when we started the engines. The storm must have opened up the bow a bit and sprung one of the kerosene tanks. It didn't seem too good a thing to have kerosene floating around loose like that in a ship that was loaded with gunpowder and gasoline.

On the morning of the thirteenth, a Friday, I was kidding the chief engineer. I had had a bad nightmare the night before and dreamed we had lost the ship and him with it; and I kept joshing him, saying that it looked bad for him. He got a little sore and told me to shut up. He didn't like the idea of joking about so serious a matter as that. Later, I was ready to admit that I didn't blame him. I don't know, but perhaps some of these old fellows are right in their superstitions. I'd be the last man in the world to violate one of them now.

That night, just at the change of watch at midnight, the chief engineer came running into my room. I heard him calling wildly, "She's gone! She's gone!" Then he rushed out of the room. Still I was only half awake and deciding it was another nightmare, I turned over and tried to go back to sleep. But just as I began to drop off I got a whiff of something burning. Then I sat straight up in bed, turned on a light and looked with horror at a lovely little grey wisp of smoke which was curling prettily around the edge of the door and making a beautiful serpentine line to my bunk. But it wasn't pretty to me. It meant that the ship was on fire and I jumped out of my bunk as quickly as I could, put on my pants over my pajamas, and pulled on a pair of boots. Then I went into the companionway where Sparks, of the radio room, was running around, jibbering about fresh water to take along in the boats. I tried to go down into the engine room but it was an impenetrable mass of black and yellow smoke which whorled up like a pot of boiling liquid. Three breaths of it would knock a man out. I dashed back on deck and found three of the crew holding the chief engineer, who appeared completely out of his head. He was determined that he would go back into the engine room and it was all they could do to hold him and keep him from sure death. Maybe my nightmare had something to do with it. Perhaps, in his panic, he had decided that he was fated to go and that he had to get back into the engine room, but they held him fast.

He kept shouting, "She's gone! She's gone!" "She'll blow up!" and, of course, every man on board believed him; it terrorized them so that they all believed it was going to happen right away.

Sparks was still running aimlessly around so I told him to send out an SOS at once. But suddenly, while he was sending the message, every light on the ship went out and his instrument was dead. Neither he nor anyone else knew whether he had got a message out before the power went off. The fire had originated in what we call the shaft alley in the stern of the ship, and the switchboard was located directly above. Something must have been burned there, some insulation destroyed, and while Sparks was sending there must have been a short-circuit. At any rate there we were without any possible means of communication and in complete darkness, twenty-three men five hundred miles off shore, in a raging ocean, with a burning ship under our feet. It's the kind of thing you always think is never going to happen to you personally. It's the sort of thing you read about in fiction, in well-planned horror stories, but it isn't a part of real life.

When the lights went out hell literally broke loose on the ship. Nearly everybody went suddenly mad. The gasoline, distillate and gunpowder were horrible specters in everybody's mind. They all thought the ship would blow up at any minute. There was no discipline, no order of any kind. They were good men, but some things will send even the best men into complete panic. The facts were bad enough but the chief's sudden hysteria was worse, as it brought every man there into the grip of terror. Then when the lights went out, something snapped in most of them and they all went berserk.

The captain was holding on to himself pretty well, but he had no control whatever over the men. I spoke to him and he agreed that we must abandon ship immediately. The fire was close to the kerosene tanks, the bilge was full of kerosene, and above it was enough gunpowder and gasoline to blow up a city.

We had about eight launches on deck which we had built to sell in Siberia, but they were heavily boarded over and chained down so we knew that we could never get one of them overboard in the heavy sea that was running. The skipper wanted to take a big barge which was on deck and try to take it to shore under sail, but I couldn't see that at all. In the first place, it seemed to me practically impossible to get it overboard in that heavy sea, and even if we managed that I couldn't believe that we would ever be able to sail the thing five hundred miles to shore, without perishing from exposure. On the other hand, we had a twenty-six-foot launch on the davits on one side which we kept for walrus hunting. It wasn't by any means as roomy as the barge and, in a way, I suppose, it wasn't so seaworthy, but we had a good chance of launching it and we had plenty of fuel aboard which we could use, if only we could get it off ship. Assuming that we could keep the engine going, we had a much better chance of making land that way than under sail with the barge.

In the blackness which surrounded us, I felt my way into my room, found a heavy coat, and started to go back on deck with it over my arm. Just as I was going through the companionway someone bumped into me, grabbed my coat from my arm and was gone.

Out on deck I tried to see what was going on. Everything was in disorder, but I found a young Swede, a fellow named Carlson, who was keeping his head and working like hell to get the launch loose, while everybody else seemed to keep getting in his way. Chief among the obstructive elements was a Russian trader named Mashikin, who was completely insane at that moment. He kept rushing around shouting wildly, "Shloopka! Shloopka!" (Boats! Boats!) "Lower the boats! The boats! Get the boats!" He ran from one man to the other, grabbing their arms, pulling at their coats, making it impossible for anyone to do anything. He came at Carlson and pulled at him, but Carlson just pushed him away and went on working. Finally, I told Carlson in a voice loud enough so that Mashikin could hear, to hit over the head with an oar anybody who bothered him.

The ship had some sail on her and the skipper set the spanker to keep her in the wind, so that we could keep the fire aft as long as possible. But obviously it had no intention of staying there long. Bit by bit it was creeping forward toward the gasoline and gunpowder, and we all knew that we hadn't long to work before there would be no deck left to work on. Even with the wind pushing the fire aft, that whale oil which soaked the ship, and the pitch pine in her, were burning so fast that nothing could have controlled the flames.

We had to have fuel for the launch and we couldn't get near the drums of gasoline. But we had all that distillate in cases and decided to take as much of that as we would need. Even so, we still needed a little gasoline to prime the engine of the launch. So the second mate, a young fellow who still had his wits about him, remembered that the launches we had aboard had all been given test runs before we loaded them and that every one of them would undoubtedly have a gallon or two of gasoline in the tank. He took an axe and smashed through the hull of one of them and retrieved about a gallon of gas.

Finally, we got the launch down and everybody scrambled to get into it—that is, everybody except the skipper, Carlson, two super-cargoes (Pearson and Schroeder), the second mate, and myself. With the launch in the water, there were still six of us left on the ship. They kept yelling to us from below that we'd better get off before she blew up, but I knew that we might as well blow up on the ship as to be adrift without food or clothing or fuel for the launch. Accordingly, we went to work as fast as we ever worked in our lives to get at the stuff we needed.

The lazaret aft, where all the ship's provisions were kept, was now barred by the flames, as were also the fresh-water tanks. So we fell upon the forward bulkhead and chopped through it to the storeroom where we kept, for show purposes, samples of trade supplies of practically everything we carried, with the exception of heavy standard merchandise. From it we snatched together a supply of heavy woolen and waterproof garments, taking everything we could lay our hands on—sox, underwear, heavy pants, mackinaws, and some guns and ammunition.

Then someone shouted that we ought to be getting another boat over, since the launch had pushed away. We lowered the small dory that we carried aft, and began bringing up the supplies to load into it. In the meantime, there it was, bobbing below us in the ocean with no one in it, ready to smash against the side of the ship at any moment. Carlson, the Swede, gave one look and jumped. It was a whale of a jump for anybody, any time, but he landed square into the boat, on all fours like a cat, picked up the oars and held it clear of the ship. While he stayed in the small boat we passed the more important supplies over the side to him—the clothing, guns, the gallon of gasoline—and he rowed to the launch with them.

There was no time to lose in waiting for him to come back for the rest of the supplies, so we dumped overboard the cases of distillate, along with five hundred-pound barrels of wienies and some cases of oranges and some of eggs; just threw them into the water, hoping that later we would be able to pick them up. Though we worked fast, the fire was outstripping us, getting closer and hotter by the second, and we knew that we must get ourselves off quickly. By this time the launch had drifted off until it was a mile or so from the ship. Carlson and the dory were nowhere in sight, and in any case we knew that it would be impossible for all of us to get into her. A whale-boat slung from the davits on the side of the ship opposite that from which the launch had been lowered seemed to be our best bet. It was lashed pretty solidly on account of the storm, so Schroeder, the super-cargo, went up to cut the lashings. But the ship was rolling so, and we were all in such a panic, that in the confusion he cut the boat-fall, too, making it impossible to lower the boat.

Fortunately, the second mate, who had helped supervise the stowing of the cargo, kept his head. He ran forward and, feeling around with his hands and feet, found a small block and tackle he remembered having seen up there. Schroeder adjusted it, we lowered the whale-boat, and the five of us managed to get into it. By this time the fire lit up the ocean, enabling us to see Carlson bobbing about in the little dory, having his hands full to keep her afloat, and in the distance the launch was still drifting. Evidently they had not yet got her engine started. We began to pick up the cases of distillate and the oranges and wienies we had thrown overboard. Altogether, we recovered fourteen cases of distillate, two barrels of wienies, and two cases of oranges. We picked up Carlson, too, tied the dory to the whale-boat, and then hung around, waiting for the launch to pick us up. By now it had drifted completely out of sight and we figured that if we tried to find it we might row in the wrong direction, whereas, if we stayed near the burning ship the men in the launch would come back to us after they got the engine started.

The fire got hotter and hotter and we had to pull away some distance from it, but we kept within the brilliant circle of light which illuminated the ocean. If it had not been our boat that was burning, if I had not had to sit there helplessly watching the destruction of a ship which I regarded as my home, and which represented a lot of planning and a large amount of money, I would have enjoyed the most thrilling spectacle I have ever seen. Even in the midst of the terrible dejection I felt as I watched it, I remember wishing that a motion picture photographer with a good camera had been there to take it. The oil-soaked timbers and pitch pine burned with a fierce white light that kept rising higher and higher. Soon the fire got into the hold where the ammunition was and there was a continuous "rat-tat-tat!" like a hundred machine guns being fired at the same time. Then the filling pipes to the oil tanks took fire. There were two forward and two aft from the house decks. With every roll of the ship, the oil, forced up through these pipes from the tanks, would spurt flames twenty feet into the night, as though they were huge gas jets.

Suddenly there was a roar and a huge mass of dark seething smoke shot up from the deck fifty feet into the air and burst into a tremendous ball of flame high above our heads. It was closely followed by another, and then another. One by one the gasoline drums were going off. Finally the flames got to the masts, and they became towering fingers, until they finally toppled into the ocean, still burning.

Suddenly Schroeder grabbed my arm and yelled, "Look!" There was terror in his voice and he was pointing away from the ship in the direction in which the launch had gone. For a moment we saw nothing. And then, as our boat was lifted on the crest of a wave, we were as scared as Schroeder. For there, out in the ocean (we couldn't tell how far away), was another fire, small by comparison with the one which was in front of us, but nevertheless a fire. It could only be the launch, the one hope any of us had of ever getting to shore. Not a man in the whaling boat was able to say anything. And then after a while it vanished from our sight.

For hours we sat in our little whale-boat, watching the *Kamchatka* burn and waiting for whatever might happen. Nobody knew whether Sparks had got his SOS out. We were somewhat off the regular course for ships and hadn't any idea whether we would be picked up or not. And, of course, while we all hoped against hope, none of us knew whether the launch had foundered or not. In the terror of that night no one could possibly have judged how serious the fire might have been. There was too little visibility, and too much interference by the high seas to tell.

About noon the next day, when we were considering the feasibility of setting a course, one of the men let out a shout that sounded as though he was going to cry. There was the launch coming toward us. The only thing that ever happened to me before which was comparable to my feeling when I saw that launch was that day when I so nearly drowned in the Sea of Okhotsk. It came chugging up to us, and the sound of the engine felt the same way to my ears as the beach had to my body when I crawled ashore. They planned to throw us a line and tow us until the sea was smoother, but something went wrong with their boatsmanship or ours, and they ran the prow of their launch smack into us. However, she was not badly stove and we soon had her patched. We decided to tow her and have the crew take alternate shifts, part of the time in the launch and part of the time in the whale-boat. We could have managed without the extra boat but the launch would have been badly crowded (as it was indeed on the one night when we all had to take to it), and we figured that our chances were better with it, even though towing it impeded our speed. Once we had serious engine trouble, we knew the launch would be useless. A whale-boat is one of the best and sturdiest of sea boats, and ours was equipped with regular whaling gear and sail. As it turned out, however, if it hadn't been for the launch none of us would ever have reached land. We would have perished from privation in the whale-boat. Speed was the only thing that saved us.

We stayed near our burning ship fourteen hours in the hope that we might still be picked up; then we cut the dory adrift and nosed away from the fire, which was still burning brightly.

When we were about ten miles away from the ship, just after dark, we saw the finish. There was one tremendous spurt of flame which, even at that distance, illuminated the sea all around us. Then the whole ocean was dark again. What we had seen was undoubtedly the explosion of the powder, which must have blown the hull to pieces, and sunk what was left of it.

By then, of course, we had heard the story of the other fire. The launch had been hanging on the davits all winter and the engine was covered with rust. The boys had taken the cylinders off her to clean them and then, to heat them up and make it easier to start the engine, they had burned some oil-soaked waste in them. Of course the whole engine was covered with oil, too, and this burned and set fire to the launch and nearly burned it up. Everything which we had feared had almost happened. But aside from a few charred spots around the engine, no actual damage was done. But it had been a night of nightmare for everybody.

The launch would have been considered a small pleasure boat on Long Island Sound or San Francisco Bay, the sort of boat on which a man and his wife might take a Sunday cruise with a couple of children and perhaps one or two guests. But with six persons on it nobody would have a very good time, because everybody would be getting into everybody else's way. We had twice that number aboard, even after part of the crew had been assigned to the whale-boat.

The engine was housed over in a little room, with space enough for one man, or at best two, to sit in a very cramped position. Forward of the engine house there was a cargo hole six feet wide and twelve feet long. We put our fourteen cases of distillate in there, with two cases of oranges, two barrels of frankfurters and one case of eggs, and then the twelve of us had to dispose ourselves as best we could.

Most of us were wet and we wanted to get into some dry things. I was soaked and began looking for all the fresh dry stuff we had brought from the ship, but I couldn't find any of it. I finally got a little rough about it and then a few sacks showed up. Some of the boys had put on all the clothes they could and had tried to hide the rest. One man had on five pairs of pants. Every man thinks of his own preservation first of all, and they were all afraid of freezing to death. I found my overcoat (which had been grabbed from my arm on the ship) on our Swedish cook, John.

But you couldn't resent that sort of thing too much. In a situation like that the best man is apt to do instinctively what he wouldn't think of doing under ordinary circumstances. As our trip went on, John turned out to be one of the most helpful men with us in keeping up morale. Mashikin, the Russian trader, was simply paralyzed with fear, and John kept kidding him about it, taunting him, "You have lots of money, you are afraid to die. I have none, I should worry." John had taken my coat and probably he also had the money Mashikin had left in his cabin.

We ran into some pretty bad weather. One time we had to heave to for fourteen or sixteen hours and during that time no one could stay in the whale-boat, so the whole twenty-three of us were forced to jam ourselves into the launch. Think of a room which is six feet by twelve and think of twenty-three persons in it—without any distillate or eggs or oranges or wienies—and you may get some idea of what it was like. We couldn't lie down. We couldn't sit down. We could just stand up, so closely packed together that if one man moved everybody had to move. Two Chinese boys who were along just gave up and lay down while everybody else stood on them. The wind and sea were so high that we couldn't run the launch. We just threw out an improvised drag anchor to keep us from drifting too fast, and let the water come over the sides, covering ourselves as best we could, and all of us worked to throw the water out of the launch as fast as it came in.

There was a lot of rust in the gas tank and the engine would miss now and then and begin to go "put! put!" as if it were going to stop. We were running on distillate and had no more gasoline. If she stopped, everyone there knew that the chances were ten to one we'd never get her started again. But through some miracle she never did quite stop.

On the fifth morning after we had left the ship we sighted the top of a little mountain peak off on the horizon. We had been steering west, and this object showed up almost due north. Nobody knew what it was, but nobody cared. It was land, and we changed our course so quickly that we almost turned the launch over as we came about. When we landed we found that it was Chernobura, or Black Fox Island, one of the Shumagan group off the coast of southwestern Alaska.

It was a little place and there was only one man on it, an old Swede sailor employed as caretaker of a blue fox farm, on which, since the island was small, the foxes were not pen raised, but allowed to run loose. The old man was none too friendly, thinking, probably, that we were a band of fox thieves come to raid the island. He saw us coming up the hill toward his house, and at first he wouldn't come out. He seemed afraid of us. I suppose we all must have looked pretty rough. Finally we won his confidence, at least to the point at which he would trade us some food for some clothing and let us get fresh water. None of us had had a drink of water since leaving the ship. We had rationed the oranges, three or four a day, and they had kept us from going mad with thirst. (And before we had sighted land we had rationed the wienies, too. It was a long time after that before I could look at a wienie again with any desire at all.)

Leaving Black Fox Island, we set our course for Sand Point, a trading station on Unga Island, where there was a wireless station. About half way there we ran into more bad weather and had to land on a nameless island which was quite uninhabited. But we got a bit of fresh food there. There were a lot of ptarmigan, and we shot them and ate them with more relish than I have ever had for any other food at any time.

We spent the night there, and then moved on to Squaw Harbor, where there is a cannery, a short distance from Sand Point. There we sent a wireless to Seattle. For ten days we waited, under the care of Andy Groswald, the local trader. Then a cannery ship picked us up and took us back to Seattle. We hadn't saved a thing from the ship. We went back with nothing but the clothes we had on our backs.

At that time we had an office in Japan and, feeling proud of the *Kamchatka,* which was one of the most beautiful ships the company had ever owned, we had sent a big picture of her to our Japanese office where it had been hung on the wall.

When I got back to Seattle I learned that the night the *Kamchatka* had burned at sea—the very night we had gone through one hell after another, Friday, the thirteenth— our office in Japan had also burned. While the ship was burning at sea her picture was burning in Japan.

Call it what you wish—I don't like Friday, the thirteenth.

Incidentally, last fall, when I drove to New York, the jinx was still with me. On Friday, the thirteenth of September, I was driving along on a beautiful highway through southern Idaho early in the morning, without a soul in sight as far as the eye could see. My daughter was with me, and neither of us saw or heard anything until we ran slap-bang into a horse. The animal had apparently been sleeping in a ditch along the highway. At any rate, the first sight that we had of him was when he made two big jumps and landed in front of the car. There was no way I could miss him and I remembered a rule of northern ice work; that if you cannot avoid an object you had better hit it straight, bow on, as a ship might be stove in by a glancing blow. In this case my car might be turned over by one, so I hit head on; killed the horse, smashed the radiator, the fenders, and the lights, but outside of a jar, there was no other damage. And on Thursday night I had promised myself to drive carefully! No use, you see.

CHAPTER XII

ALMOST immediately after returning to Seattle from the ashes of the *Kamchatka,* I left for Japan to pick up a Russian ship, the *S.S. Tungus* (named after a tribe of Siberian natives), and proceeded to the Sea of Okhotsk to finish up the business I had started to do aboard the *Kamchatka.*

We worked along the coast until we came to Okhotsk itself, and there we ran smack into the Russian revolution. The remnants of the White navy had just taken the village with their fleet, which consisted of two tramp steamers and a little gunboat. They found the Reds in charge and they had only one round of ammunition for the guns on the gunboat, but they fired that over the village, then landed four hundred troops equipped with obsolete guns, and a band. By the time they got to shore the Reds had all taken to the woods, so the Whites marched up the street with the band playing *God Save the Tsar* and the place was theirs. There was no bloodshed, no opposition of any kind. The Whites just marched in and settled down.

We also landed without any difficulty, after the White officials had boarded our ship, gone carefully through all of our papers, and collected a lot of revenues from us.

There were about a thousand Korean miners there and some Russian placer miners. Everybody seemed to have a little gold, so we traded merchandise for gold as well as for furs. The miners would bring the gold in and after weighing it, we accepted it as currency for whatever was the mar-

145

ket value. We kept it all in a stout canvas bag. Before we were ready to leave we had over $14,000 in gold.

Captain George Stavrokov, one of the owners of the ship, was with us, and a young Russian, Mark Grinstein, who was one of the smartest traders I have ever known. Grinstein and I spent our time ashore, trying to clean up our business as quickly as possible, for the future looked none too bright, with the hills full of Reds and a feeble force of Whites holding the village. We wanted to get away as soon as we could.

I think we stayed there three days and then were ready to pull out. We had already taken most of our things down to the launch which was to take us back to the *Tungus,* and Mark and I were cleaning up a few things at the house, when Captain Stavrokov came up and said that General Polyakov, commander of the White forces, was down at the launch and wanted to go out with us to go aboard his own gunboat. But Mark had a few things still to clean up. There was one fellow who owed us twelve dollars, another fifty cents. Mark was determined not to leave until he had collected. He made a couple of trips down to the launch with some more things and then came back to try to collect that $12.50. I asked him what he had done with the bag of gold and he reported that he had given it to the second mate, who was in charge of the launch, so that was all right.

But when we finally got down to the launch, really ready to start, we found that it wasn't all right at all. The launch, the second mate, General Polyakov, and the bag of gold were gone! Some of our own boys were on the beach looking rather confused and helpless. They told us that Polyakov had commandeered the launch because his little gun-boat had been in some bad seas and his own launch had been washed off the davits and lost. He had originally intended to give us a ride back to our own ship, but he finally got tired of waiting for us. He was roaring drunk anyway, and had suddenly pulled out his gun, pointed it at the second mate, and shouted, "Full speed ahead!" Even when the second mate did his best to obey, the general had not been satisfied. The tide had fallen and the mate was having some difficulty getting off the beach and Polyakov, thinking someone was holding the painter, suddenly went wild with rage and fired a half dozen shots at the end of the painter, narrowly missing some of the boys on shore.

We sat down on the beach and all of us looked a little foolish. There we were, eager to get away, with the *Tungus* riding at anchor ready to take us. But we had no way to get to her. And even if we could figure that one out, there was our perfectly good launch and our bag full of gold, gone—to say nothing of the second mate. None of us said anything about it for a little while. Then we all got up and went back to the house to wait.

For over four hours we sat around talking about it and no one had a good word to say for the revolution. Finally, we all lay down on the floor and went to sleep. At four o'clock in the morning a young White Russian lieutenant, a couple of soldiers, and the second mate came in and woke us up, telling us to get a move on and they'd take us back to the boat. We didn't waste any time asking questions.

As soon as we were outside, walking down the beach in the dark, the second mate, Mark and I got a little ahead of the others so we could talk.

"What did you do with the gold?" Mark whispered to the second mate.

"I put it in the shaft alley," the other answered. "I covered it up with an old bag."

"Where is it now?" Mark went on.

"I suppose it's still there," the mate answered. "I didn't see anyone take it."

"Like hell it is!" I exploded. I couldn't imagine $14,000 worth of gold lying around without someone discovering it.

The mate argued that it must still be there, Mark began to bawl the mate out, and I defended the mate. We got so interested in the talk of the gold that we took no notice of what was going on around us.

But we were brought up sharply by the sound of guns firing not sixty feet away and the whizz of bullets about our ears. We threw ourselves flat on the ground, but the shooting went on over us, followed by angry shouts in Russian: "Halt! Stand on the spot!"

As we had already halted and were even then lying on the spot, the order seemed superfluous. We were all wondering whether the young White Russian lieutenant had simply chosen this way to dispense with the necessity of explaining about the launch and the gold. But just then four soldiers emerged out of the darkness ahead of us, demanding in Russian, "How many wounded?" Before any of us could answer, another volley of Russian broke out, this time from the young lieutenant in our rear:

"If anyone has been wounded, I, personally, shall cut your hearts out with my own hands," he shouted to the four soldiers, who saluted him as he came up and began to explain. They were sentries, and had been posted there with orders to let no one pass. They had ordered us to halt, they said, but we had paid no attention. Probably they told the truth. We had been so busy talking about the bag of gold that we couldn't have heard anything.

As we continued along the beach, the second mate told us what had happened on the launch. He had been ordered to take Polyakov to his gunboat and had done so. Here Ivan, one of the Russian engine room men, and another fellow left the launch, taking some of their stuff aboard from shore. Then the launch had proceeded to the *Tungus,* the second mate had been kicked off without ceremony, and the launch had started back to the gunboat. But the skipper of the *Tungus* was a Russian, Captain Krakmalov, and when the mate told him what had happened, the captain went to the bridge and began blowing the whistle of the *Tungus:* "Toot! Toot! Toot!" one blast after another without stopping, until the launch turned and came back. Then, speaking in Russian, the skipper had pleaded with Polyakov's men to let the launch go ashore again and take us off, which they finally agreed to do.

But we still knew nothing about the gold, nor whether there was any intention to compensate us for the launch. I wasn't worried much about that. I figured that I could take it up with the Russian Government later and get some redress but I knew that it would be pretty hard to prove how much gold there was in that sack or whether one of the Russian crew had taken it. I knew the Russians needed gold badly just then, too. I decided that if we didn't get it back right away, we wouldn't get it. I told Mark how I felt about it and he, with a greater confidence than mine, said, "Leave it to me. I'll get it back or know the reason why."

All the way back to the ship I could see Mark in the stern of the launch feeling about here and there, whispering to the mate, and I could hear the hoarse, excited whisper of the mate's answer. But just before we got to the *Tungus,* Mark came to me.

"It isn't there," he said in disgust. "Try and get them to come aboard with us and I'll go to work on 'em."

"You can't start anything with the Russian Army," I replied, pretty sore by then.

"I don't mean that I'll take a punch at anybody," he argued. "We've got better ways than that."

So I got them all aboard and told the cook to bring us the best supper he could scare up on such short notice. We all sat down to food and plenty of vodka. Mark kept urging them to drink, and I found a few presents; some fur mittens (which were better than anything the Russian Army issued), cigarettes, and plenty of tobacco for all of them. In an hour they were all pretty drunk and we all relaxed and had our arms around each other's shoulders like traditional brothers. Then Mark went to work. Up to that time we had been afraid to say anything about the gold, for we thought we might be telling them something they didn't already know, and which would only put our chances further off.

Mark had picked out as his particular friend, a tall, good-looking Russian named Mishka, a soldier who had been all

through the revolution, a chauffeur for Simioneff, and a
noted character among the Whites. It was obvious that he
carried himself with considerable authority among his fellow soldiers, and that he would be a valuable ally.

I saw Mark, very depressed, sitting next to Mishka with
his head in his hands and Mishka seemed deeply concerned.
When he asked what the matter was, Mark began to cry.
He did it beautifully, too, with big tears rolling down his
cheeks and his mouth all screwed up so that he looked like
a baby whose candy has just been taken away from him.

"That big American," he whimpered, pointing at me,
"is going to kill me if I don't get that gold back."

Mishka looked puzzled, but he was not one to let his
friend down.

"What gold?" he asked. "Where is it? I, Mishka, will get
it for you."

"I don't know where it is," Mark sobbed. "I put it down,
and it's gone. I was responsible for that gold with my life."

Now Mishka's arm was about Mark's shoulder, and he
was patting him gently as one might soothe a child, and
through the looseness of his face which his semi-drunken
state had brought, shone determination and the bright light
of devotion to a friend. So Mark, seeing that it would be all
right, told him the whole story.

Mishka's eyes lit up and he smiled brightly.

"Oh, that gold!" he said. "I know where that gold is.
Ivan's got it. Come with me. I shall cut out Ivan's heart!"

Mark, who was, of course, perfectly sober all the time,
followed Mishka without hesitation. Going out, he leaned

over swiftly and whispered in my ear:

"For God's sake, keep the lieutenant here until we get back."

The other soldier followed Mishka while I gave the lieutenant another drink and talked fast about everything I could think of which would interest him. I enlarged upon what a fine looking lot of men he had, asked questions about the army's recent occupation of Okhotsk, and got him to describe other victories. I heard the launch chugging away from the side of the boat, and I was half on my toes with nervousness for the hour I sat there drinking and talking with the lieutenant. Then I heard Captain Krakmalov tell the engineer to get up steam and take in the anchor.

Meanwhile Mark and Mishka and the other soldier were on their way to the gunboat, cementing their friendship with vows of eternal fealty, and Mishka was telling Mark how he knew that Ivan had the gold. But Mark still didn't know what would happen when they got to the gunboat. They couldn't go to General Polyakov. For one thing, he was in a drunken stupor, but even if they could make him understand what it was all about, they would probably be worse off than before. The Whites needed gold badly and the general would probably take it with no more compunctions than he had shown in taking the launch.

But Mishka had no intention of going to the general. He knew his Ivan and how to handle him. They went aboard the gunboat as quietly as possible and directly to the engine room, where they found Ivan asleep. Mishka went straight to him, shook him roughly to waken him and, still holding onto him, said, "Where is it?" Ivan never said a word. He just lay there shaking like a leaf and, reaching under his pillow, pulled out the bag of gold and handed it to Mishka, who passed it on to Mark.

Then they all came back to the *Tungus*. By that time the lieutenant was practically out. But it was a simple matter for a crew who were used to handling sacks of flour and bundles of fur, to load him onto the launch without bothering to tell him good night. Then, almost before the launch —which had once been ours and now belonged to Russia— was on its way back to the gunboat, the screw of the *Tungus* was turning and we were headed away from there.

CHAPTER XIII

You might have thought that anyone who had run into a revolution, as offhand as that, and who had been warned by events, could have kept his nose out of trouble, but the following year (1922) I was back along the coast of Kamchatka in the motorship *Mazatland*. By then the Whites had gained control of the whole coast. The victory which we had seen General Polyakov win with his little gunboat and 400 troops had been only the beginning of a series of similar victories. We were in a country still torn by the revolution, but definitely in White Russian hands. Five years after the revolution had been successful in Russia proper, it looked as though it still might be a failure in Siberia.

We found Kamchatka full of Russians who had come up there with the Whites, and almost overnight we changed them, in appearance at least, into Americans. It was really striking and amusing. There was a shortage of clothing in Russia just then and most of the natives needed everything from hat to shoes; we sold them corduroy breeches with lacing on the legs, American high-topped leather boots, mackinaws—they loved dark blue ones especially—and American caps. We could scarcely get our merchandise unloaded before they rushed to buy it. They would come to us in sheepskin coats and astrakhan caps, looking like the Russians of picture books, and go away looking like American prospectors or ranchers. Years later I ran into some of that

154

clothing in Moscow. In 1922, it was so hard to get clothes in Moscow that people bought things from me in Siberia and sent them home to their relatives.

When we went through the Customs we had been assigned some supervisors, White Russian army officers who were to stay with us and see that we did everything according to their regulations. One of them was a priest whom I shall never forget. And it was through this priest that we made friends with a number of White officers and, in a small way, became an unwilling part of the revolution itself.

We had worked our way up the coast to a place called Gizhiga. It was a difficult place to get into because of the tides and the ice. We had to lay up about eleven miles from shore and go in with the tide. As we went in I noticed a young Colonel in charge of a group of White Russians unloading a boat. What took my attention was the fact that he was not standing off to one side simply giving orders, the way most army officers work. When I first laid eyes on him he was in the icy water up to his hips, giving the men a hand at a difficult spot. I decided right there that he was one of those rare leaders who wouldn't ask his men to do anything he wasn't willing to do himself.

I was introduced to him and he invited me to dinner aboard his ship. His name was Bochkarov and he was the commander of the White forces along the entire coast. He was thirty-two years old, had been a Don Cossack, and had learned all there was to know about recklessness and butchery. Yet he talked like a gentleman and seemed a kindly fellow to me.

I was thinking about this at dinner that night when one of his men came in and reported that a soldier had stolen a watch from one of the sailors. Without the slightest hesitation Bochkarov ordered the watch returned to its rightful owner and the thief was to be shot on the spot. It made me wonder a little what he was really like. I don't think I ever found out, although I got to know him fairly well. I saw him in many diverse situations, heard him reject proposals to shoot offenders with as much alacrity as he had condemned the man on his boat, saying, "This shooting business is no good," but I never felt as though I really knew him.

That night, when I left the ship, I was accompanied by another like him, a Colonel Fielkovsky. There seemed to be nothing to talk about and I started to whistle an old Russian song that I liked—*Time Will Change and Your Heart Will Find Peace*. Suddenly I noticed that the Colonel was crying like a child. I stopped whistling.

"Whatever is the matter?" I asked.

"That was my mother's favorite tune," he said.

I didn't know what to say. I knew that Colonel Fielkovsky had a reputation for being as courageous, as unthinking of himself in the face of danger, as hardboiled, and, on occasion, as brutal as Colonel Bochkarov, whom I had just heard order a man shot for stealing a watch; yet here he was, weeping like a three-year-old child over a song his mother used to sing to him. Then he told me about his mother.

He had been in the cavalry of the Imperial Guard in Moscow when the revolution broke out. One night his doorbell rang and he opened the door to find a closely veiled woman standing there. He didn't recognize her and he never learned who she was.

"Go away at once!" she whispered to him.

"Why?" he asked.

"I can't tell you, but please go away—quickly," she urged him, laying a hand on his arm in pleading.

"Who are you?" he asked, and tried to take her hand, but she snatched it away and ran swiftly down the steps and into the dark.

He went into the living room where his mother and father and sisters were assembled and simply told them that he was going out, without mentioning what had just happened. While he was away a mob of Reds came to his house and asked for him. When no one could tell them where he had gone, the Reds shot them all—father, mother, and sisters. It was in the early days of the revolution when there was undoubtedly a great deal of stupid, unauthorized bloodshed, and Fielkovsky's family just happened to get in the way of some of it.

"How could I ever be a Bolshevik after that?" he asked. "They killed everything that was dear to me. I know they'll kill me, too, but I'll kill every Bolshevik that I can as long as I live."

Fielkovsky, Bochkarov, and the priest we had on board with us, all felt the same way about it. They all knew that they were fighting for a lost cause. And they also knew that they would be killed sooner or later. It was only a question of time. But the only thing they seemed to care about was to die fighting, to eliminate as many as possible of the hated Reds who had destroyed their world.

The priest was one of the best two-fisted, card-playing, hard-drinking men I have ever known in my life, and a devil with women. Just what his official position was I don't know, but he was much more like an army officer than a priest. He seemed to have the same amount of authority and was given some of the most responsible jobs to carry out. And he did them as well as Bochkarov or Fielkovsky would have done.

There was a time, before he was on our ship, when Bochkarov had caught some Reds in the hills near Okhotsk. The prisoners were put on a gunboat with the priest in charge. Officially, they were to be delivered to headquarters. But before the ship sailed Bochkarov called the priest aside and said, "Don't land them." As I have said, the priest was a man like Bochkarov, one who would ask no one to do something he was unwilling to do himself. So, as soon as the ship got out to sea, the priest lined all the prisoners up against the rail and took out his revolver. As he faced each man he said the same thing: "God may forgive you, but I never shall!" Then he shot the prisoner dead. One by one, he shot the whole lot of them with his own hand, and with his own hands pushed their bodies overboard. That is the kind of man he was—the kind that whole group was made up of.

We tried to carry on our regular trading business, but the revolution didn't care much about the importance of the fur traffic and was constantly getting in our way. We were dealing with the natives at Okhotsk as usual, and were about ready to leave the place when the officer in charge there came to me with a proposal which was very like an order.

"We're having difficulties here," he said frankly, "and I want you to help us. There are ninety men here that I want you to take down the coast and land for us—I don't care whether it's east or west, so long as you get them out of here and land them at least two hundred and fifty miles away."

"I won't do it," I told him. "I'm conducting a peaceful and legitimate business in furs and I'll not take part in your revolution."

"Do as you like," he sighed. "But if they don't get out of here there's going to be trouble, a lot of fighting, and you'll lose your ship. Besides, you've got a lot of furs ashore and I'll make it my business to see that you never clear with them even if you do get your ship out."

There was an American vice-consul on board our ship at the time and I tried to pass the buck to him.

"What shall we do?" I asked him.

"We?" he answered. "This is your problem. There's nothing I can do about it. You'll have to fix it up some way yourself."

I thought it over and decided that I'd have to make the best bargain with him that I could. I knew that the officer who had approached me could commandeer the ship if he wanted to, as he had done with other vessels. So I went to him and told him that I would take civilians away if he wanted me to, but not soldiers. I told him that I was going to Petropavlovsk and that if he wanted to send unarmed men with me all right, but that I would let no one on board who had a gun. He agreed to that and we took his cargo of men aboard, searching them and their baggage as they came on. We found only one shotgun, which we kept. We landed them all at Ola, two hundred and fifty miles up the coast. One of the men was Mishka, the man who had helped us recover our gold the year before.*

Meanwhile, Colonel Bochkarov was having a counter-revolution in Gizhiga. His band, the one which had played *God Save the Tsar* whenever he landed victoriously at a

---

* In the early spring of 1924, a man dropped into our office in Seattle. His face was only vaguely familiar and at first glance I had difficulty in recognizing him; but when he smiled I placed him as the same officer who had commanded us to take the ninety men aboard our ship on account of the trouble they were having in Okhotsk. Naturally, his civilian clothes were a great contrast to the snappy uniform of the Colonel of the Imperial Guard. He had got away from Okhotsk on a little gunboat, he said, and finally reached Shanghai. From there he went to San Francisco and then to Seattle.

He apologized for the inconvenience he had given us through his order at Okhotsk. He had learned later that it had thrown somewhat of a political significance on our operations, and he had come in to make restitution for the wrong he had done us, saying that he did not understand conditions at the time, and was sorry.

He told me he had heard that our stations were under arrest and subject to confiscation. Realizing that he was in a way responsible for this, and wishing to correct his blunder, he made me the following proposition: "You have a small motor schooner, the *Chukotsk*, that has fair speed and does not require a large crew," he said. "Put a navigating officer and an engineer on board and I will get ten of my men and we will go up north and make the points along the coast where your goods are under arrest. We will bring all of your furs out, and perhaps some additional furs, enough, at least, to partially cover the losses you have sustained."

Though his sincerity was obvious, of course I could not accept his proposal. I thanked him very much for his kindness and generosity in offering it but made it plain that I could not go into such a venture. Getting mixed up in a revolution was bad enough, but to go into outright piracy was a little out of my line. Technically, his scheme was entirely feasible and could have been successful, particularly at the isolated points where some of our stations were. If I had been living in the good old days, say a hundred years ago, and such a proposal had been made to me, I would probably have accepted it as grand sport.

A few years later I again saw this colonel. He was in the uniform of the United States Army, and had become completely Americanized in his ideals and his thoughts.

town, for some reason or other decided to do away with him and join the Reds. One day he was coming up the river in a launch with a young soldier at the tiller when some of the members of the band, lying in ambush on shore, fired on him and killed the young soldier. This was one of the times when Bochkarov's sentimentality showed itself. He kissed the boy, who had been with him a long time, told him good-bye, and took the tiller himself. The firing kept on and he was shot in the arm and easily captured.

His captors put him on board a schooner and, not knowing that we had landed men at Ola, decided to take him there. Some of these men saw the schooner coming in and Mishka, dressing himself as a native, went out to the launch in a skin boat to see what he could see. Looking through a porthole, he saw Bochkarov with his arm in a sling. He paddled back at once, of course, and told his group about it.

They waited until dark, then they rushed several native huts and armed themselves with rifles. When, a little later, a landing party came ashore from the schooner, the boys were ready for them. They killed the landing party, took the launch back to the schooner (which they captured without difficulty), then set sail, returning to Gizhiga with Bochkarov and recapturing it. One of Bochkarov's first acts, after the reoccupation of Gizhiga, was to have a priest named Koch, who was one of the instigators of the revolt, taken out and actually skinned alive.

But of course the Reds got Bochkarov in the end. He was sitting in his house one night with his wife when a group of Reds broke through his lines and threw a bomb through the window. He came out at once with his hands in the air.

"Do anything you want to with me," he said, "but don't kill my wife."

They told him that all they wanted him to do was to run. He started to run and they shot him in the back and killed him. But that was the end he expected, the end he had been approaching all the time. He knew that they would treat him that way when they caught him. It was the kind of treatment he had given them. Whatever atrocities may be charged against the Reds, at least as many and as horrible ones can be charged against the Whites.

The revolution changed the life of everybody in Siberia, just as it did in Russia, but it was a different kind of change. The Tsar's government paid little attention to the Siberian native. He did his trapping and his trading and there was no governmental interference of any kind. The natives, even though they lived in what we might call poverty, and under conditions of filth and ignorance, were free to live and do business as they chose. But when the Reds took over the country and declared a monopoly, they changed all that, for both the native and the trader. The government confiscated all business and fixed prices. Fur prices dropped from an average of between seventy-five and ninety per cent of retail market value to about fifty per cent. The natives couldn't get a decent price for their year's labor and they couldn't obtain the merchandise they wanted and needed.

All of the people with whom we had been dealing were used to a selection from the widely varied stock of merchandise we always brought with us. We brought them foodstuffs, canned milk, canned fruits, clothing of every kind (including frilly things for women), hardware of all kinds, toys for children, a great many luxuries which many of them had never known before. Now, with the Soviet monopoly in force, they got only such things as the Soviets saw fit to send them, and the government showed less imagination in its selections than we had done. Luxuries were completely taboo and the natives had to content themselves with a pretty grim, dull selection of absolute necessities, and not too many of these. There is no question that the standard of living in Siberia dropped sharply and promptly as soon as the Soviets came into power there.

In 1923, the Bolsheviks cleared the remnants of the Whites out of Siberia and promptly proceeded to take over everybody's business, including ours. I had reorganized and was operating under the name Olaf Swenson and Company, and Olaf Swenson and Company in Siberia was now in the hands of the Soviet government. Everything that we owned there, physical properties, merchandise, furs, and money, was taken out of our hands and held by the government— properties which represented an investment worth substantially over a million dollars. They didn't call it confiscation. They said the properties were "under arrest." There was a warrant out for my arrest, too. I never did find out why, even when I finally was arrested. But it was apparently the result of some of the things my competitors had said about me, some of the men who had suffered because I had dealt fairly with the natives and gotten along with them better than they had done. There were stories that I had been selling guns to the Whites, some of them rather amusing, in face of the facts. In those days you could start out talking about an air gun, and in five minutes it would turn into a fourteen-inch howitzer.

I met R. S. Pollister, vice-president of our company, in Harbin, China, and together we went to Pekin to see Kara-kan, the Soviet ambassador. We finally got a visa from him and went to Habarovsk, the capital of Siberia, to see the head of the G.P.U. there, in an effort to get him to remove the "arrest" from our properties. But he didn't seem to know what it was all about, so we were forced to go to Moscow.

For months we went from one government official to another, but no one seemed willing to take the responsibility of lifting that arrest. First, we had to take care of taxes. According to their way of figuring, there were taxes to pay for six years back. They wouldn't take our statement of what business we had done, and what our profits had been. They insisted on using their own estimates. They decided that we owed them 660,000 gold rubles, which was the equivalent of about $340,000. We kept fighting that and finally got it down to about $62,000.

We agreed to settle for that amount. But then came the difficulty of the merchandise which was under arrest. They wanted the merchandise. They had a business monopoly. They wanted to take over the merchandise and sell it, crediting us with eighty per cent of their receipts against our taxes. The same thing was true of the furs. We had a tremendous stock of furs which they also wanted and there was nothing we could do about it. I sold one parcel of furs to them for $161,000. A month later I bought them back for $190,500, and was then allowed to take them out of the country. It was legalized confiscation. They simply took a profit of $30,000 out of that one lot of furs because they were in a position to do so. They had learned from the Tsarist government, I suppose, that "might makes right" and now they were in the saddle. The proof that the price they paid me in the first place was too low is in the fact that, even buying them back for $30,000 more, I still sold them outside at a profit.

The thing that was hardest to bear was the fact that all the time this was going on—months and months—all of our merchandise was deteriorating. Thousands and thousands of dollars' worth of it was completely spoiled. A lot of it was "lost," a convenient word which covered a great many disappearances.

And, of course, most of the money which was owed to us just disappeared, too. We had been doing a large credit business. It had been our custom to pick out a local spot, put a good man in charge there, and finance him against the business he would do for us, letting him operate under his name and extend credit according to his own judgment. He would advance our merchandise to natives at the beginning of the season and they would bring him furs in payment for it when they had collected them. During all of our arguments with the Soviet government, which consumed practically a year, our books were sealed and we couldn't get at them. Then the Soviets put through a decree cancelling all debts incurred under the Tsarist regime, and no one owed us any money. Some of them paid no attention to it, of course, and paid up. But for the most part they did what anyone would do anywhere—they simply didn't pay, and we were out of luck. But we had to pay the money we owed other people. The decree did not affect our responsibility. We had a lot of Russians on our payroll and their wages went on and on and we had to pay them.

Then suddenly it was open season for lawsuits against us. We were foreign capitalists in a country in which the worker was the law and suits were filed against us right and left. Everyone who sued us figured that, in the new worker's courts, we wouldn't have a chance.

We were sued by a man who lost his eye through fooling with a rifle which belonged to us. The rifles were a part of the merchandise which was being held "under arrest" by the government, and a government workman was going through the merchandise, taking inventory. We had nothing to do with it. The workman took a 22-calibre rifle and thought he would find out whether it would work. He didn't close the breech properly and when he pulled the trigger, the shell flew back and put out one of his eyes. So he sued us.

Another man claimed that he had sent some furs to us at Vladivostok and that we had not paid him as soon as we should have, so that he had been forced to spend the entire winter waiting in Vladivostok. He made out a long list of items on an expense account which he kept while spending the winter there, including all it had cost him to live, and added the value of the fish he might have caught and the furs he might have collected had he been at home. Then he sued us for the total. But we proved to the court that he hadn't stayed in Vladivostok on account of us at all. He had bought a new launch and had been unable to get it on the steamer in the fall, as there was no room. He had simply waited around until spring so he could take his launch home with him.

However, we won every one of the private suits against us. The courts were admirably fair. Even though they were set up by, and composed of workers, they saw through the absurdities which were presented to them and rendered just verdicts.

During this time I had to go to Vladivostok to take care of the fellow who was trying to charge his winter vacation to us. When I arrived there I was arrested. I had just got settled into my room at the hotel when a Soviet policeman, or soldier, walked in very abruptly and glared at me as though I were the sole survivor of the old White army.

"You're arrested!" he grunted.

"All right," I said, "what do I do about it?"

"Where are your documents?" he asked.

"They're downstairs in the hotel safe," I told him.

"Give me your gun," he demanded.

"I have no gun," I told him.

"You've been to Harbin and back here and back to Harbin again," he said accusingly. "What have you been there for?" Then without waiting for an answer to his question, he again demanded that I give him my gun.

I was losing my patience a little. If I was under arrest, that was that. I was perfectly willing, anyway, to face any court on the record of what I had actually done and been in Siberia and Russia, and after my experience with the new Russian courts I was not too worried about the situation. But I didn't relish standing there and having meaningless accusations hurled at me by this whippersnapper who didn't know what he was talking about, and seemed intent only on being unpleasant.

"Look here," I said, "if you want to ask me questions, ask them like a gentleman and I'll answer them like a gentleman."

His sneer was calculated to put me forever into my place.

"We have no gentlemen in Russia any more," he said, and the sudden flare of defiant pride in his eyes equalled the sneer of derision on his lips.

"You are excellent evidence of that fact," I said.

By then the manager of the hotel and the bookkeeper had arrived. The manager stood behind the other and made motions to me which I didn't understand then. Later I learned that he was simply stalling for time, trying to keep the officer there as long as possible while one of his clerks downstairs got the prosecuting attorney (a friend of the manager's) to go to headquarters and get things fixed up.

"Perhaps you'd better take an inventory of the room," the manager suggested.

"Go ahead," I said. "Inventory everything. Lock it all up if you want to. Practically everything else I own in Russia is locked up anyway."

The officer thought that was a good idea and spent a lot of time getting the room sealed. Then we started downstairs together. It was silly, I suppose, but the one thing I was worrying about as we went down was the embarrassment of walking down the middle of the street to the police station. I don't know how it is now, but in those days, when you were arrested, you couldn't ride. You couldn't even walk on the sidewalk. You walked down the middle of the street in the custody of an officer, and everybody knew you were under arrest. I hated the humiliation of it, especially as it was such a dirty day outside, raining, and the streets were covered by a thick filthy slush.

"Could we get a cab or a droshky?" I asked him.

"When you're arrested, you walk," he said stiffly.

"I've done a lot of walking," I said. "I've gone through deeper slush than this. I guess I can stand it."

He made no reply, but strangely enough, just as we left the sidewalk a droshky came by and he hailed it. So we rode to the police station after all.

Here we marched up to the door and stood ourselves before a little slot which opened so that an officer inside could see who we were. The first thing he did was to indulge in a string of abuse against the man who had arrested me for bringing me there in a cab. They argued about it for five or ten minutes, calling each other every dirty name I have ever heard. Then the fellow inside talked for a long time to someone else on the phone. He turned to me.

"You can go," he said, "but first you must sign this document."

He shoved some sort of paper at me, but I didn't take time to read it.

"I'll sign nothing," I said. "I want to know why I have been arrested."

But he would answer none of my questions.

"Just sign this document," he said, "and then you may go."

"I'll sign nothing," I repeated.

"All right," he said, "then you may go anyway."

As I turned away, the fellow who had arrested me brushed by me and ran half a block to get me a cab. Then he opened the door for me and bowed me in as though I were one of the Commissars.

What it was all about I don't know to this day. The prosecuting attorney came to see me at the hotel and told me that there had probably been a mistake made in names, but even he wasn't very clear about it. People were just arrested in those days, and sometimes shot—and explanations were made later, just as Negroes are lynched today in the southern part of the United States. Everything was upside down. Mistakes were made and sometimes people were killed but they were just as dead, when the Soviets found that they were wrong, as they would have been had their executioners been right.

There was something pathetic and admirable and frightening about their fervor. It was hard for anyone who had always lived as Americans live, without any need for revolutionary tendencies, to understand them. I have never seen such passionate sincerity as some of the young communists showed.

Later, under more favorable circumstances, and when things had settled down a little, I got to know them better. During the winter of 1931, when we were stuck in the ice on the *Nanuk,* we had a bad time with our mixed crew of Americans, Scandinavians, Irish, and Germans. Everybody got in the way of everybody else, and we were so bored and irritated by each other that we were ready to throw marlin spikes.

About two miles away from us the Russian ship *Stavropol* was also ice-bound. But they were having a beautiful time, with no trouble at all. Every morning at eight o'clock classes would start. Those who were illiterate were learning how to read and write. Others were studying foreign languages or engineering. Sometimes they would come over to our ship and borrow a part of an engine, or something like that, for a demonstration, and we would send an engineer over with it to demonstrate it. They even studied astronomy.

At another time I was going overland with a reindeer team and overtook a man walking along, carrying a shotgun. As I came up to him I saw that he had a little strip of paper in his hand. First, he would look at the paper and then look away and mumble something to himself. I discovered that he was a local secretary of the Communist party and was going from one village to another. I gave him a ride to where our paths diverged and noticed that he was still looking at his slip of paper, then turning away and mumbling.

Finally, I asked him what it was all about and he showed me. He had written down about two hundred Russian words, with their English equivalents, and he was trying to learn English that way. I don't believe he had the slightest idea that he would ever go to England or America. He just wanted knowledge. So from there on I helped him with the pronunciation of English words and we had a good trip.

But this is all getting ahead of the story.

We finally settled directly with the government on a common sense basis, avoiding court action wherever we could.

They had our merchandise. They were in power. I had had
a lot of experience in handling Siberian furs and Siberian
natives and I wanted to continue in business. Each of us
had something the other needed and I knew that spilled
milk was never regained by crying over it. So I made a deal
with them, settling all of our difficulties, and entered into
a joint trading venture with the government. I think that
I was the only American who settled with them on the spot
in that way, thereby avoiding years of legal difficulties, with
the consequent winding and unwinding of miles of governmental red tape.

At first we made a contract for a year. Then, in 1926,
after the first year's contract had worked successfully, we
made a contract for five years, in conjunction with Albert
Herskovits and Sons, and with Cantor and Angel, of New
York, whereby we would bring American merchandise to
the Soviets according to their own specifications from Moscow, turn it over to them on a cost-plus basis (including, of
course, a reasonable charge for delivery), and they would
turn over to us all of the furs from the territory assigned to
us, also on a cost-plus basis.

During those years the Soviets lived up to their contracts
meticulously. In spite of the financial ruin and the months
and months of difficulty which the Russian revolution
meant to me, I have no complaint to make against the Soviet
government.

CHAPTER XIV

As A result of the five-year contract which I made with the
Soviet government, in 1926, by the terms of which I was to
bring supplies into Siberia and take out furs collected by
the government from the natives, I purchased the schooner
Nanuk and for two years made successful trips with her
along the Siberian coast. During this time we had no trouble
with the ice, as both years were open seasons. During the
first, we made the run in two months and twenty-six days.
In 1927, we made the same trip in the *Nanuk* in two months
and nineteen days. We were beginning to think that our
luck with the ice had changed permanently.

In 1928, together with my associates, Maurice Cantor and
Irving W. Herskovits, of New York, we left for London and
made two additional contracts with the head of the Soviet
Fur Trust, which necessitated additional floating equipment. As a result of this, I went to Norway and purchased
the *M.S. Elisif* as there was no ship available under American registry suitable for Arctic work. The *Elisif* sailed
under the Norwegian flag to Seattle, took on a cargo of supplies, and with Captain A. P. Jochimsen as Ice Pilot and
R. S. Pollister in command of the expedition, sailed for
Cape North, where, on the 22nd of August we became fast
in the ice, about eleven miles from the Cape.

The next day some natives from the Station arrived with
a skin boat and some dogs, for they were out of supplies and
wanted to take with them what they could. They also

brought a letter from Kavelin, the Gostorg representative, who was also impatient, but for another reason. He was simply bored to death with Cape North and wanted to finish his business and get back home. He asked that I come to the Station and inspect the furs.

To give you an idea what a cargo of furs is like, I will tell you what this collection which Kavelin had waiting for us comprised. There were:

<pre>
1896 white fox
 400 blue fox
 135 red fox
   6 cross fox
  27 polar bear
   6 brown bear
2869 reindeer fawn
1610 pounds of ivory
2638 hair seal
      miscellaneous smaller furs
</pre>

The young Russian cook at the station, and the trading agent gave us the best the place afforded in the way of food and beds. There were six of us at the station and only one three-quarter bed, and although Smirnoff, the agent, offered me this, I hadn't the heart to take it. All the time that our boats were along the coast, we had visitors, and it was quite impossible for us to give them beds without sleeping on the deck ourselves and running the chance of inheriting from them a great deal of vermin. So, when I, in turn, became a guest, I found that my conscience would not let me take any better than I felt able to give. Consequently, I slept on the floor with a beautiful polar bearskin as mattress, another one for a blanket, and a large wolfskin rolled up for a pillow. I did not get much sleep for I discovered, after a few hours, that I was full of corners. I never realized before how much my elbows and hips seemed to stick out or how hard are the skull and claws of a polar bear.

The young Russian fed us well on rolled oats and reindeer soup, but he felt that the soup was a little too lean so, while it was boiling merrily, he put a couple of large spoonfuls of lard into it. I couldn't quite understand this until I was told that he was only acting as cook but was really an engineer, and I suppose he had become so used to oiling engines that he simply couldn't keep away from the nearest lubricant when he started to make soup.

There was a great deal of talk at the station about the prospects of the ice breaking up, but no one seemed to have much hope that it would do so. Smirnoff and another Russian were so sure that the ice would stay that they were planning a trip of two hundred and seventy-five miles along the coast, in order to catch the Russian steamer, *Tomsk* (which was due at East Cape, two hundred and seventy-five miles away), by September 20th, to take them to Vladivostok.

After spending two nights at the Station, we went back to the boat, where we settled down and watched the ice, driven by a strong southwest wind, speculated on the chances of its breaking up, shot a few geese, and listened to stories told us by natives who came aboard. Meanwhile, it was impossible for us to discharge our supplies or to take on our furs.

It began to look as if we might have to winter there, but

our position was so bad that I was reluctant to give up hope, even though it was not well founded. About two hundred miles west of us, the Russian steamer, *Kolima,* was in the same predicament as we were, and reported to our wireless operator that she was making all preparations to winter there. The *Stavropol,* fifty miles off Wrangel Island, reported scattered ice.

There would be little danger to the ship until the break-up the following June, when there was a grave possibility that she might be shoved high up on the beach by the ice moving inshore. But this same movement promised safety for any of the crew which we left on board. A ship is not likely to be swept out to sea by the ice on the Siberian coast, because of the prevailing inshore winds. A crew caught in an ice break-up has no difficulty walking ashore, whereas, on the Alaskan coast, the currents and drifting ice are prevailing offshore and frequently move at the rate of a mile and a half, or two miles an hour, so that a crew, staying with an ice-bound ship during a break-up, may be carried far to sea. Or, if the crew abandons the ship too late, they are likely to be carried off on foot, since they are unable to travel over the rough ice as rapidly as the ice is traveling seaward.

After a week, we finally broke through the snarl of ice about us and got under way. But our feeling of triumph was short-lived. It took us four hours to get our bow swung around so that we could proceed at all, and six more to cover a distance of eight miles to a point about three miles offshore, where we stuck fast again.

Here we unloaded as best we could, the ice greatly ham-

The Russian ship, *Stavropol*, frozen in so that ice and snow completely covered her decks. The lower picture is a view made after a southerly wind had formed an open lead near the ship

pering the movements of the barges on which we sent our cargo ashore. The natives were interested in our plight but not very hopeful that we would be able to proceed. One of them told us that a baby had just died at the Cape, which meant that very bad weather was ahead.

Whether the dead baby had anything to do with it or not, I don't know. But the indications that we would be able to get out diminished rather than increased and I began to speculate on the possibilities of going back to Seattle without the ship. There were two ways of doing this. One was to fly out over the narrow and hazardous strip of water which separates the Siberian from the Alaskan coast. That had little appeal for me. Although the distance is not over thirty-eight miles by air, the trip is an extremely hazardous one for planes, due to the strong wind-currents and blizzards, and, therefore, as we learned through radio communications with a commercial airline in Alaska, tremendously expensive. Aside from that, I suppose that one of the reasons why this method had so little appeal for me was that it seemed rather unexciting.

On the other hand, there was a way to get out which no white man, nor anyone, so far as I know, had ever tried. Forty-five hundred miles away, across vast expanses of uninhabited tundra, frozen rivers, and steep, almost inaccessible mountains, lay Irkutsk, a station on the Trans-Siberian Railway. I had had so much fun on my dog-sled trip across Alaska that I thought a trip ten times as long, over unknown and difficult country, might be ten times as much fun.

I went ashore again and talked it over with Kavelin. He

decided that if I went, he would like to go along with me as far as his own home, a village several hundred miles away. It was an unheard-of thing to do. It never had been done before and we knew that the mere task of getting together enough dogs and equipment to make the trip seem feasible, was a huge task in itself. So, still undecided, still hoping that after all the ice would break and let us out, I went back to the ship and waited, getting as much entertainment as possible from our native guests.

One of them whom we had aboard was deaf and dumb. All the others treated him with a strange respect and awe. They said that he had died and come back from the land of the dead. After his resurrection, he was deaf and dumb, because the spirits did not want him to tell others about the silent land to which he had been. What the basis for the story was I never knew. Perhaps he had suffered a stroke of paralysis from which he had only partially recovered, and through which he had lost his speech and hearing. But to the natives he was little less than a god.

Another native, Aletet, who was with us, seemed to be making the ship his permanent quarters. He lived at a nameless village which was on the route we would take to Irkutsk, and, learning this, I began to cultivate him. He would be an admirable, potential asset, in case we decided to move overland.

There was a young Russian aboard with us whom we called "The Catsup Kid," because he consumed about two bottles of catsup a day, spreading it thickly on bread as though it were jam and calling it delicious. He spent much of his time studying English from my dictionary and decided that our language is full of flaws. Why, he asked, do we use two a's, one right after the other, when one will do? I told him I could not think of any words in which this happened and he proudly showed me the first word in the dictionary—"Aaron."

Day after day it snowed and I watched it with mingled depression and excitement, for if we decided to go overland, early snow would mean an early and a good trail. Even before I made up my mind definitely that it was hopeless to wait for the ice to break, the crew were busy preparing quarters for winter, building bookcases and decorating their cabins.

The natives began asking for alcohol, but they didn't get any, for there was none on the ship; nor would they have received any if there had been, for natives and alcohol do not go well together. They seldom get liquor, but they have a good substitute.

Once, in my early days of trading, while stationed at Anadir, a number of natives came aboard in an unusually jovial mood and I thought they were drunk. Still I knew there was no liquor on the boat and I asked one of the sober ones where they had got it.

"Wapak," he answered.

I had never heard of such a place so I asked him to explain. It developed that it was not a place at all, but a mushroom found in some parts along the coast, especially at Cape Navarin. The effects seem similar to those of alcohol but there are no bad after-effects. It relieves pain, but the natives use it more for the stimulation it gives them than for anything else.

I asked one of the natives what he felt like when he had wapak in him and he said that his legs were "too light" and that he could see a louse a mile away. He offered me some, but I told him that I could see lice a damned sight closer than that just then without any wapak.

Early in September there were several days during which the wind blew an icy gale. When it ended the sea was locked in ice as far as the eye could reach. There was no break anywhere. Looking out across it one morning, I gave up hope that we could get out by water and began to make active preparations for our trip overland.

First I commissioned a native to build me a sled.

There are no sleds on earth which are stronger or which will take more punishment than those made by the natives of Siberia. The best of them are made of hickory and oak, put together entirely with rawhide lashings. There is not a screw nor a nail anywhere. This construction gives them an elasticity which withstands an unbelievable amount of strain, whereas sleds rigidly constructed, with the joints made fast by nails or screws, are likely to break, while traveling rapidly, when they come in contact with cakes of ice or frozen hummocks on the tundra. Also, the rawhide lashings facilitate repairs when a part does break.

A native sled is a beautiful example of balance and fitness to its purpose. It is not steel shod, but the wooden runners are carefully tapered to the front, thickening toward the middle, which makes them pliable. Stiff runners make the sled much more difficult for the dogs to pull, and steel runners freeze and stick to the ice. Steel is better for early fall and late spring when the runners may break through the snow or where the snow is so scant that a great deal of gravel is encountered. For our purposes I had steel runners put on the sled for the early part of the trip when the snow would be thin, and I planned to take them off later, when we got into deeper, harder snow.

When a sled is ready to go, the natives soak the runners in warm water and let them freeze. Several times during the day when traveling, they are iced with a small piece of reindeer skin, soaked in warm water and drawn swiftly along the bottom six or eight times, leaving six or eight thin layers of ice on the working surfaces.

The only serious drawback to traveling with a wooden sled is that you have to carry a bottle of water inside your parkey, or skin shirt. When you are out of water you fill the bottle with snow and put it next to your skin to thaw it out, which isn't a very pleasant thing to do in temperatures of fifty to sixty degrees below zero (Fahrenheit).

I also engaged native women to make clothes for me—a parkey, and some sealskin pants lined with Hudson's Bay blankets, and some mitts and socks.

Meanwhile, the men of the crew were finding entertainment with the natives, too. One day a native slicker came aboard looking for an easy mark. He had the skin of an Arctic hare, to which he had very carefully and skillfully sewed the tail of a white fox. He knew better than to try to sell this worthless combination to a trader, but he bided his time until he had made friends with a member of the crew, who knew nothing at all about furs. Then, getting the man aside, he produced the skin. The sailor looked at it with envy, thinking of a girl in Seattle who would be grateful for a beautiful white fox skin, so he asked the native how much he wanted for it.

"You no got small bottle whiskey?" the native asked.

"Me got," the sailor said immediately with complete assurance.

As I have said, there was not a drop of whiskey on the boat, but the sailor was a fast worker and as much of a slicker in his small way as the native was. So he hurried to his quarters where he had an empty whiskey bottle, with nothing left in it except a few drops and the aroma. Quickly he poured these few drops onto the cork and filled the bottle with cold tea; going back, he let the native smell the cork, urged him to hurry ashore before someone saw that he had whiskey. The native was delighted, the sailor was delighted, and everyone was happy, especially some of the other boys who knew enough about furs to see exactly what it was that the sailor had got for his bottle of cold tea.

Perhaps our most difficult job in getting ready for as long and arduous a trip as we were planning was to get enough good dogs. I have thought of this a number of times since when people have asked me what a good sled-dog is worth. It is absolutely impossible to place a price on a good dog, especially if he is a leader. Buying one is almost like buying a human being who is going to undertake a joint venture with you. You know that before your trip is over the dog may have saved your life by his intelligence, instinct and courage. It is he and his team who will often lead you through a snowstorm when every guide which you have has failed. Many a time when I have been on the trail, fighting my way back to camp through blinding, driving snow, I have turned the job completely over to the dogs; they could smell the way to camp, pick up an old trail which even a native would be unable to find, and bring me safely in. Sometimes, when you are traveling on ice and the sled breaks through, a good leader who minds instantly and accurately, will get you out without difficulty, whereas a poor one will simply increase your hazard and, likely as not, send you to your death. This is the kind of dependability on which it is impossible to place any market value. You try to find the animals that you want, that you can believe in and depend upon, and once you have found them, you buy them (if you can) for whatever price you can arrange.

I shall never forget Billkoff (Snowball, in English), the finest dog I have ever known, any more than I can ever forget the best of my own friends who are now as dead as Billkoff. I met him many years ago when he belonged to a native, and I wanted him ten minutes after I had seen him. It was not only for his record as a leader, but his personality, his character, and his wisdom. These things are as evident in the finest dogs as they are in people. I made friends with Billkoff, and while he was courteous to me, he always remained on his dignity, too. A working dog in Siberia has none of the insipid, fawning tricks of a pet house dog. He has a dignity which is frequently unapproachable, and Billkoff had this to a high degree, yet we came quickly to respect each other, and I found myself wanting him more than I had ever wanted any other dog. I tried to buy him but his native owner had as much appreciation of a good dog as

I had and would not sell him. Completely courteous, however, he would never come out frankly and tell me that he thought too much of the dog himself to let me have him, but always gave me another reason, saying, "I don't think that dog would be any good for you. He is too used to me. He wouldn't mind anyone else."

I gave up then, but when I came back the following year I found that I wanted Billkoff as much as I ever had, and offered his owner a higher price. Still he refused, insisting that he didn't think Billkoff would serve me well. I raised the price two or three times until I had got it far above the average native's wildest dreams, but Billkoff's master, although he looked more and more confused and wistful every time I raised the price, insisted that Billkoff would do me no good. Finally, although I would willingly have paid even more than I had offered, I stopped bidding because I could see how deeply attached the native was to the dog and what a terrific conflict I was setting up in his mind by the extravagant offers I had made. It seemed cruel to make him suffer longer. As a matter of fact, I admired him greatly for his loyalty to his dog. I left him, and admiring him as I did, went out of my way a little later to do him a small favor. After that I did not see him again until the following year. When I went to call on him and Billkoff, with no intention of again trying to buy the dog, the native walked out to greet me. Then going over to Billkoff, he took him by the collar, led him over to me, and placed my hand on his head.

"Your dog," he said solemnly.

Surprised and, of course, delighted, I tried to pay him but

he would have none of it. He had been unwilling to sell the dog to me but now he felt that there was only one way to repay me for the favor I had done him, and that was to give me Billkoff.

When I started out to work with the dog, I discovered that the native's spoken reason for not selling him had been more than a stall. For six months he was the worst dog I had ever known. He simply refused to accept me as his boss and constantly took matters in his own hands. Finally, however, he gave up the struggle and from then until the day he died (several years later) he was the best dog I had ever seen in any man's team.

When we were on the trail, with Billkoff leading, there was never any trouble. I could put into the team the most stubborn fool cur in the world, the kind of a dog who will tangle the whole team by refusing to follow the leader; but when the leader was Billkoff, he had only to take command, go to the right or to the left, and every dog in the team would follow him, so that they acted and looked like one unit. It was automatic—it was something that Billkoff had —more than any other leader I have ever seen.

One of the great troubles with dogs on the trail is that they have a tendency to go wild if you happen to scare up some game. They all want to leave the trail and follow the game. But we could pass fox, or wolf, or reindeer with Billkoff in the lead and you would think that he had never seen the animal. And if we were lost in a storm, he would use any available means to find the trail and stay on it.

I remember once when we had been hauling wood over a trail for quite a distance. We had with us a fellow named

Bill Witleson, who chewed tobacco all the time, and as we went along the trail between the wood supply and the camp, Bill would spit tobacco juice every hundred yards or so. One night we got caught in a terrific blizzard after dark, miles away from camp, where we were driving in with a load of wood. I was completely helpless, without any means whatever of finding our way. But Billkoff settled down with his nose to the deeply fallen snow, and without any apparent difficulty, found his way from one spot to another, taking us into camp along the tobacco trail Bill had left for us.

There is a mysterious relationship which exists between the leader and the rest of a dog team. Through some subtle evidence of power, a dog takes leadership and becomes king of his group. He rules them with an iron will so long as his kingship lasts. He will fight to retain his crown and win his fights, and all of the other dogs respect him. Then one day another dog will best him in a fight and take over the throne, and from that moment on the former king's leadership is gone. Once licked, he is licked forever, and will run yelping from the smallest and least significant cur in the whole group. I suppose it is from this, as much as from anything, comes the expression, "Every dog has his day."

But Billkoff's day lasted until his death from old age. He is the only sled animal I ever had who frequently shared the house with me. He could do everything but talk, and in his own way, he did a little of that, too. I would say something pleasant to him and he would look up at me and grin as plainly as any human being. And even when he became too old to do much work, and spent most of his time lying around the house, he still remained king of his group of dogs. No other dog ever attempted to fight him. When he would come out among them, they would run up to him and lick his face and show the plainest evidence of affection and respect, and Billkoff would sit in their midst, his head high, looking at them with kingly dignity. I don't think he ever realized, until the day he died, that he had reached the point at which any one of those young dogs could have whipped him in a physical fight.

When you realize that there are dogs like Billkoff in the world, and on the other hand, dogs which just hold you back on a trip rather than help you, you can see that it is impossible to set an average price on a team. As a matter of statistical fact, I have paid as high as one hundred fifty dollars each for good dogs, and found them hard to find, whereas I could have bought all the ordinary animals I wanted for ten dollars apiece. But in addition to the element of need for a good team over a long trip, there is the matter of fun. Driving a good bunch of dogs is the best fun in the world and driving a poor team, the most exasperating.

In picking dogs, you look for speed and pep. When a good dog gets a command to go, he wants to move as much as you want him to. He seems to enjoy it, and a good team will jump like one animal to the pull of the sled. It's a beautiful thing to watch and a fine thing to feel in front of you. But when you get a bunch of bums who pull in a dozen different directions, who have no unity and take no joy in their work, it's just punishment from start to finish.

But regardless of a dog's spirit, he has to have a good body, too. Good feet are important. A lot of the dogs that are offered for sale in the north have poor feet, worn down by long trails, thinly padded and likely to become so sore on the trail that they will have to be carried on the sleds. And when your sleds are already so heavily loaded that you are walking yourself to save the dogs, it puts murder into your heart when you are compelled, not only to diminish your dog power, but to add to the load of the remaining dogs by giving a cripple a ride.

A dog also needs good flanks, to give him the stamina necessary on long pulls. Sometimes, in high, freezing winds, we would cut deer skins into strips, wind them around the flanks of our dogs, and knot them over the backs, to keep the thinly furred flanks from freezing.

And strangely enough, in a country where good dogs are so important, the best are not produced by selective breeding. Only some of the Russians and some of the most prosperous natives in the largest villages, make any attempt at breeding to standards at all. By far the largest number of the natives take their pups as they come, raise them, train those which look as though they might amount to something, and do their selecting after the dogs have actually proved themselves, rather than before they are born. You can't tell anything about a sled animal by his looks. Some of the best looking dogs are the most worthless, and some of the poorest looking curs you ever saw are the best dogs in harness.

When I first went to Siberia and began buying dogs, I decided that I wanted a sporty-looking outfit. I made up my mind that I would have a white team, composed of especially large, fine, well-matched animals, with fine red harnesses and red sleds. I was going to be cock of the trail and show those natives how fine an outfit could look. I could see that the natives were amused, but they hunted up the dogs all right, and I got my white team. It looked like a million dollars. It would have made the most impressive exhibit any department store could have ever imported to amuse the children at Christmas time. But as a sled team it was no good at all. There were a few good dogs in it, but before long I replaced half of the team with dogs which had stamina and speed and intelligence. For years the natives kidded me about that white team. They'd laugh and say, "Swenson wants a white dog. He doesn't care whether it's good or bad; he just wants a white dog."

You can tell whether a dog has stamina or not by feeling his back. If the vertebrae stand up higher than average, if the depressions between the knobs are deep, you may be pretty sure that you have a dog that will stick to the trail day after day without playing out.

All of the natives train their young animals to some extent. When a pup is quite young a rawhide lashing is put around his neck and he is tied up with a team and made to follow, so that he will get the swing of it. The Karakees, who have some of the best dogs in Siberia, put their pups in a dugout underground as soon as they are born, and keep them there, in the dark, until they are ready to put them to work. Then, when the dogs are brought into the sunlight for the first time in their lives, they are so delighted that you can't hold them back.

All of the natives train their teams to a certain gait by keeping the loads on their sleds to about the same average weight all the time. Once that weight has been put on a sled they will not add another pound, for a heavier load will break their gait and ruin their performance. They are very careful about their feeding, too. An overfed dog will not work. The natives feed them only once a day and then sparingly, a little seal or walrus meat, and a small piece of blubber every day as a laxative.

At night they are chained out of doors. It seems cruel at first glance, but the dog's welfare, as much as the master's, is at stake. A dog loose at night will chase anything which comes around—a wolf, or fox, or deer—and wear himself out. And the dog, as well as the wolf or fox, is likely to be caught in a trap or lost. If they are taken into the house at night, the frost with which their fur is loaded will melt, and the next day they may freeze to death or take cold and come down with pneumonia. And they don't suffer at night out of doors. Their fur is very heavy and they make nests for themselves by turning about in the snow. If you are stormbound on the trail you always try to get your dogs on the lee side of a cake of ice or a rock, or something which will break the force of the wind.

As I watched the native women making the fur garments which I was to wear on the trip, and I saw how fine they were, I wondered how much valuation the customs authorities would place on them. One of the petty annoyances which I always had to face on my trips was that of customs inspectors. After paying duty on a cargo of hundreds of thousands of dollars' worth of furs, it always annoyed me to have to declare a few personal belongings which I had picked up, or this or that which had attached itself to the ship.

Sea lions on the shore, Kamchatka

In 1925, for instance, along the Siberian coast, two squirrels swam to our ship and climbed up the anchor chain. No one had any idea where they came from or what they were doing in the sea, but they seemed so grateful to have something solid under their feet that they settled down and decided they would stay on ship. The crew built a big cage with a wheel in it and became so fond of them that when a Russian trader offered us two more as a gift, we accepted them and the boys found a great deal of pleasure in taming them and watching the four of them at play.

When we got ready to clear for home, a Siberian customs official held us up at the last minute, demanding an export duty of ten dollars for the squirrels. I figured the squirrels were actually worth about a dollar each, basing my appraisal on what their pelts were worth, but he, when I asked how he arrived at the figure of ten dollars, said that since the law said nothing about squirrels, he had classed them as live stock and that if I would not pay the ten dollars duty, I would have to leave the squirrels on shore.

A trifle annoyed at this, I went to the squirrel cage and opened the door, whereupon the animals immediately ran out and scrambled up the rigging. Two of them balanced themselves on the ball at the top of one of the masts; the other two did a graceful tight-wire walk on the stays between the masts. I went back to the customs officer.

"All right," I said, "go catch them and keep them on shore. I'm damned if I'll pay ten dollars duty on them."

The officer, after one look up the masts, reduced the duty to fifty cents for each squirrel, so I paid him.

But duty or no duty, the clothes which were being made

for me were beautiful and I began to feel proud of them long before they were finished.

Then came the night when we knew that our job there was finished. We had assembled the countless materials which we needed for a trip across forty-five hundred miles of frozen tundra, bleak mountains, and uninhabited river bottoms, a trip which no human being had ever made in its entirety before, and went to bed for the last time on the *Elisif.*

CHAPTER XV

FINALLY, on the nineteenth of October, we got away. The party consisted of four dog teams; Mishka, a half-breed Chaun boy; Kavelin, the representative of the government trade organization "Gostorg;" two natives with dog teams hauling grub, dog feed, and other supplies; and myself. We had planned our trip to follow the coast through Nizhni Kolymsk, then strike across country to Verkoyansk, and, turning there to the south, go through Yakutsk and follow the general course of the Lena River, with horses, into Irkutsk.

Our equipment was in excellent shape and I knew that we had good dogs. The only thing which worried me was the presence of Kavelin; he was timorous, not particularly robust physically, inexperienced in such extended hazards as those which we were about to undertake, and, generally speaking, not the kind of person you would choose for a traveling companion on a trip like this. But he immediately settled down on a sled, wrapped himself up in his furs, and disappeared from view, emerging only now and then to ask me what time it was. I didn't mind at first, but after taking off my mitts a dozen times that first day, in temperatures well below zero, pushing back my fur cuff and looking at my wrist watch, I began to resent it. As the trip progressed and the weather got colder, his persistent habit of asking for the time became the major trial of the trip, until I was tempted to tell him that I had lost my watch. But I didn't really realize how greatly I was annoyed at it until we had finally reached his village and I learned that he had been carrying a watch of his own all the time, and had asked me the time simply to save himself the annoyance of baring his own hands in those icy temperatures. I tried to get him to leave the sled and walk and run beside the dogs, as I did, to stimulate his circulation and get himself into condition for the hard days and nights which were to come, but I could not budge him. He simply retired into his furs—his face, on those rare occasions when any of it was visible, a mask of misery—and resigned himself to suffering throughout the trip.

Our first objective was the village in which was the home of Aletet, the native who had been on the ship with us. He had promised to go on with us from there, with two or three dog teams, as far as Chaun Bay. We made it in two days, having traveled an average of about thirty-five miles a day, and immediately sent two of our dog teams back to Cape North, since we expected Aletet to replace them. However, we found that Aletet was not there and that he was not expected for a week. To all of our inquiries about him the natives answered simply, "Ko," which means literally, "I don't know." But it means much more than that in native communication. It really means, "Maybe I don't know, and maybe I do, and if I do I'm not going to tell you." It is the most common answer which a native makes to questions asked by a stranger. They are hesitant to give any information about one of their number to anyone they do not know, and will almost invariably answer requests for such information with a monosyllabic "ko."

We were in a bad position, without enough dogs, and short of dog feed for those which we had. And the natives were not disposed to furnish us with either to enable us to go on without waiting for Aletet's arrival. Finally, Kavelin threatened them with some sort of official government action and that worked. They produced two dog teams and two natives, and we started off again.

The second morning away from the village we were awakened by the arrival of a party of natives, who turned out to be Aletet and two of his friends. He seemed very much excited and very eager to ingratiate himself with us. He said that he had arrived back at his village just a few hours after we had left it and that after having heard all the *pungel,* he had immediately started out to follow us and square himself. What had probably happened is that the natives, hearing Kavelin's threats, had sent a dog team after him to bring him back. At any rate, when Aletet reached us he seemed very eager to be in our good graces and arranged to have two dog teams accompany us as far as Chaun, and he gave me four good dogs in exchange for four mutts which I had.

At Cape Yakan, we were held up by a blinding blizzard for three days and spent our time in a native hut. By native standards, it was rather large and a good one, with a *yorrung* about 10 x 14 feet, and the house itself about twenty-five feet in diameter. As is usual in native houses, the *yorrung* was living room, bedroom, dining room, kitchen, sleeping room and toilet, all in one.

Despite the size and comparative splendor of the place, Kavelin and I decided to sleep in the outer part of the house to escape the unbearably fetid air of the *yorrung*. We both had wolf-skin sleeping bags so the cold didn't bother us, but the stench was terrible. After the eight or ten natives who lived there had stripped off their parkeys and subjected their bodies to the heat of three seal oil lamps, the air was much too rich for us.

The lady of the house was tanning deer legs for a pair of fur mitts, or more properly speaking, softening and scraping them, and we relieved the tedium of our wait by watching her. First she chewed the skin with her teeth, softening it and dampening it so that it would not break while scraping. Then she worked it with a scraper made of a curved piece of wood, about two feet long, with an iron washer set in the middle.

Her daughter, a girl of about seventeen, took care of the water by putting ice in kettles which hung over seal oil lamps. No wood fire was used in cooking. When the kettles boiled we had tea. There was no particular time for it—it all depends upon the condition of the lamps.

Twice a day we ate raw frozen meat and topped it off with a bit of boiled meat before going to sleep. The natives eat with their fingers and their knives. Taking a piece of meat between their teeth, they hold the other end with their fingers and then cut a piece off by passing the razor-edged knife between their lips and fingers. I wondered how often their noses and lips were slashed off, but I never saw any signs of it.

Since the weather made seal hunting impossible, one of the natives spent most of his time hunting lice. Taking his shirt off, he would go over every inch of it. We could tell when he was lucky by the click of his teeth as he popped the louse into his mouth. They say that lice are sweet to the taste and very good, but I never was quite willing to find out for myself.

The young lady who made and served the tea, was naked except for a pair of very abbreviated tights. At times she would run into the outer house to bring in a piece of meat or ice, but she did not bother to put on any clothes even then. It's marvellous how they can stand the cold. And they have absolutely no sense of physical modesty. Their imaginations are uncomplicated and they simply would think it funny that anyone should want to hide his body.

The naked young lady carried an extremely dirty cloth with her and, before pouring tea, wiped the cup out with the cloth. If there was a spot in the cup which would not come out, she would spit on it before applying the rag.

Their dishwashing was a simple process. The girl who served simply licked the dishes clean with her tongue. The meat platter was shoved under the deerskin curtains where the dogs performed the same service.

One of the children had a running nose. Whenever it got to be too bad his mother simply leaned over, placed her mouth over his nose and mouth, and took care of it with her tongue and lips.

I could not begin to describe the filth in which these people lived. One of the squaws had so much dirt on her back that it could have been scraped off with a blunt knife. They had no soap, and when, on rare occasions, they wanted to wash their faces, they used their own urine as a solvent.

When the blizzard subsided we left Cape Yakan, pushing against a strong northwest wind which constantly blew fine sharp snow into our faces and eyes.

To add to our difficulties, our Primus stove refused to work, so that the first morning out our breakfast consisted of native tea and cigarettes, and we had no lunch. Consequently, when we reached the native village at night and were taken in and fed a big supper of seal meat, we ate it in spite of the way it was served. The hospitable squaw who fed us paused just before giving us food to wring out the baby's diaper (a handful of moss); without even having wiped her hands she handed us the meat in them. You might think that we could not have eaten it, but after a day such as we had just gone through on the trail with no food, it made less difference than you might imagine.

Three days later—in other words, nine days after we had started the trip—we washed our faces for the first time at the home of a Russian trapper named Gregory, who lived in a comfortable sod house, and who gave us a taste of civilization again. Some of the old timers say that it is better not to wash your face at all while on the trail, as an accumulation of dirt protects the skin from cold. But I like to wash mine at least once a week and to shave, too.

The comfort of a clean-shaven face in the Arctic becomes something much more than a matter of fastidiousness. A long beard may look fine when you want to send a snapshot home, but anyone who actually wears one for long on the trail in the Arctic does so at the cost of pain and unpleasantness. Inevitably, the beard becomes filled with snow and frost and tiny icicles form in it, and I know of nothing more unpleasant than trying to pick these out. Further, if you crawl into your sleeping bags at night with an icy beard, the ice thaws and you get all wet.

At Gregory's house we took the steel runners from the sleds and iced the wooden ones. Up to that point we had been driving over a somewhat spotty trail, in which there were frequent soft and sandy stretches, across which the steel runners carried us much more easily than wooden ones would; but by the time we were ready to leave Gregory the weather had turned colder. It promised a hard trail over which iced wooden runners would serve us much better than steel ones.

We lost a little time at Gregory's through the fact that finding a comfortable, decent house again, I decided to sleep inside. When I awoke in the morning, my sleeping bag and clothing were soaking wet with the accumulation of water from thawed frost, and I had to dry them out. The most important rule in winter traveling is to keep your clothing and your dogs' fur as dry as possible, and this can be done only by not allowing the frost and snow in them to thaw out.

As I was drying my clothes Gregory told me about three Russians who had lost most of their dogs a year before through disregard of this elemental rule. They had stopped there in a blizzard with thirty-six dogs. Intending to be good to the beasts, but, as it turned out, actually being cruel to them, the men had brought them into a shed overnight. Here the frost and ice in the fur thawed out, but there was not sufficient heat to dry them, so they started out the next day with wet fur. The temperature dropped rapidly and, by night, only nine of the thirty-six dogs were alive. The rest had frozen to death.

Our plan had been to press on as rapidly as possible even in bad weather, because of the shortage of dog feed. The wind shifted to the north and increased in velocity so that the snow, driven before it, became an impassable curtain, and we decided to stay another day. It was not a pleasant prospect, as our dogs were rationed for a quick trip to Chaun Bay, and there was no feed to spare along the coast, since the natives were having a hard time rustling enough for their own needs. But we had no choice.

Traveling along the coast line in any blizzard, or even on a black night, is always dangerous on account of the precipitous bluffs along the shore and the fact that in many places the ice breaks loose, making it necessary to detour around large expanses of deep, open water where a misstep may kill or cripple some of the dogs, or break up the sleds, even if all the men escape duckings and broken legs and arms. So we sat and waited and talked with Gregory and his wife.

Meanwhile, the wind veered and the blizzard increased in ferocity. I began to worry about the dogs, which were chained outside, as usual. On the second morning, I got up at five and went to see how they were. They were in such a bad situation in the storm that I loosed them all and took them into the storm shed, regardless of the trouble I knew it would be to get them dried out later. I was afraid that, if we left them where they were, we would lose them all. The wind was so strong I had to fight it every inch of the way, leaning against it, and falling all over myself when a sudden lull would catch me off balance. The snow was drifting so badly that it was practically impossible to keep one's eyes open and I had to feel my way with my feet to where the dogs were.

The snaps on their chains were so thoroughly encased in ice that I could not unsnap them with my clumsy mitts on. I took the mitts off and tried again, but it was no use. My fingers stuck fast to the frozen steel and it was only through shaking them vigorously and yanking them off forcibly that I could free myself from the grasp of the frost. My fingers felt as though I had just taken hold of a piece of red hot iron. Finally, I cut the dogs' collars, as the only way I could get them loose.

One of the dogs had been lying in the same spot all through the night and did not get up when I called him. Once or twice he tried, but he was helpless and finally gave up. Running my mitt under his body as far as I could, in an attempt to lift him, I found that he was frozen fast to the ice which had formed under his warm body. By chopping away some of the ice with my knife, and cutting some of his fur in the process, I finally managed to free him, leaving a large patch of fur where he had been lying.

I have lost dogs by having them snowed in so thoroughly in a blizzard that they could not burrow out. Sometimes I have not found them until the spring thaw. That's one of the reasons why I always keep them tied up now. If you know where your dogs are you can dig them out after a blizzard.

Perhaps it was in the north that the phrase "a dog's life" originated, for certainly the poor beasts know more of the trials and hardships of life than they do of its joys and comforts. Yet their lot is no harder than that of their masters. The lives of both men and beasts are strange cycles of contrasting feasts and famines. Both men and dogs at times go for days without eating. The only advantage which a man has is that he can tighten up his belt a notch when he is hungry. But the dog has neither belt to tighten nor understanding of the causes of hunger.

Gregory told us that a year before we were there twelve dog teams were caught in a blow near his place which lasted twenty-three days without let-up. With food enough for only a few days, most of the dogs starved. Those which did not were killed for food. The poor Russian priest who was with the party lost most of his prestige, for although he prayed day after day that the blizzard might end, there was no cessation of it.

The only places where famine is unusual are those in which they have plenty of fish. The more energetic of the natives dry or smoke fish and store them for the winter— the rest simply dig holes and throw them in as they are. These latter are called green fish. After they become ripe they are green in color as well as in name. Thawed out, you have to eat them with a spoon. But though fish in this condition are obviously putrid, there seems to be no bad effect from eating them.

Frozen fish are not at all bad food. The freezing seems to make them lose much of their unpleasant flavor. When a frozen fish is served it is placed near the fire just long enough to thaw the outside. Then shavings are cut off. One traveler, coming back from Siberia, reported that the natives ate wood shavings.

Dried fish make ideal dog feed when traveling. But not only humans and dogs eat fish in this country. Horses and cows in Kamchatka love them. I once saw a horse steal a live fish from under the nose of the man who had just caught it and, holding the head between his teeth, run away like a mischievous child, the tail of the fish flapping against his head.

I don't particularly care for the milk of fish-fed cows, since it has a definite fishy taste, but the natives don't mind it. As a matter of fact, anyone who objects too strongly to the flavor of fish in this country would go hungry, for it is in everything—seal, walrus, bear, eider ducks, and even in milk.

Anyone who lives here for long becomes accustomed to a number of odors and flavors which are objectionable at first. Many of them actually become unnoticeable. When you first come up here you can smell a native before you see him, but after a while you see him first.

While we waited for the blizzard to pass I talked with Gregory and some of the natives to satisfy my curiosity on a number of points. We talked about the habits of fox and walrus, about native customs, and about the moot question as to whether there is any undiscovered land still in the Arctic.

Although Roald Amundsen or other explorers never found any on their trips over the pole, I believe that there may be some undiscovered islands north of the Siberian coast. Millions of geese go north in the spring and return in the fall. Droves of mice leave the coast and return. Fox leave the coast line after the freeze-up and return. Of course, fox can live on the ice, so this has no particular bearing on the subject. Yet their movements have all the marks of a migration. Trappers along the coast report a noticeable exodus about the middle of November and a return about the middle of March.

A native from Cape Yakan was carried off on the ice a number of years ago and returned safely after three weeks. He reported sighting land, but did not go ashore for fear of finding hostile tribes there. Of course, he may have sighted Wrangel Island.

Finally, after four days as Gregory's guests, rather pleasant days on the whole, except for our impatience, we got away again. The wind was still blowing sharply, but the snow had packed firmly before it, so that we had good going.

CHAPTER XVI

As we left Gregory's place, I couldn't help being amused by Kavelin. He was so huddled up in his furs and double pants and double coat and triple shirts, all bundled together by a belt, in which he carried a big revolver, and even further hampered by a big box containing a lot of papers of some kind which he insisted on carrying under his arm, that I began to forget I had been irritated by him. With all his impediments it really would have been impossible for him to run or walk, as he should have done, and so I made no protest this time as he bundled himself up on the last sled, so that the other sleds would break trail for him, and started off.

After a little while we hit a river which I knew flowed into Chaun Bay, toward which we were heading. The ice was crystal clear and under it we could see the water flowing onward to the sea, so that by following the direction of the current, we knew that we would come to the Bay without trouble. We also had the advantage of smooth ice under our sleds. As all rivers do in hilly countries, this one did considerable twisting and winding about, so that while our general direction was northwest, in following the river we might for a little while be traveling directly southeast. Theoretically, of course, traveling a twisted trail like this adds a good deal to the distance. But we were in an unknown part of the country. Even the natives who were with us knew it only approximately. And added to the danger of being lost should we leave the river, was the fact that on any other trail we would have had to go over mountains and not only add the long uphill pulls to the work of our dogs, but encounter bad snow. So we simply stuck to the river. But Kavelin, it developed, had a compass with him, and every time we would turn away from our course, he would stir himself enough to get out his compass and begin shouting frantically that we were going in the wrong direction. He became almost panicky about it as if he thought we were kidnapping him, but neither the natives nor I paid very much attention. By then I decided that he had to be treated as you would treat a small child, and I simply was as patient with him as I could be, and we went on.

About noon we ran across an old native wandering forlornly about the banks of the river, going from one side of the river to the other, apparently looking for something. He was very old and seemed very distressed, and when I asked him in his native tongue what was the matter, he told me that he had lost his bedroom. The night before he had bundled himself up for sleep in his rather fragile hut. During the night a big blow had come up, so that when he opened his eyes in the morning he found that instead of looking at his ceiling, he was looking at the sky. His house had simply blown away from him without his knowing anything about it. The natives who were with us told him who I was and he immediately forgot all about his lost house and began to beg for tobacco, sugar and matches.

About tea time we came to the hut of a native who said his name was "Kom in Whats." He wanted to go across country and was just waiting for someone to come along, so that he would not have to be alone. He seemed to know quite a little about the passes through the mountains, so we gladly added him to our party.

That night we camped on the trail and were off again at daybreak in a heavy snowstorm which greatly hampered our progress. Late in the afternoon we saw five dog teams in the distance, and so hungry were we all for news that we turned off the trail and tried to catch them, but they were going too fast for us. However, when we reached high land, one of the party looked back, saw us and waited until we came up with them. One of the natives in that party and one of ours simultaneously shouted, "Rapungel." And then we came together and told each other everything we knew of any interest, including, of course, such important items as the old man who had lost his bedroom and Kom in Whats' destination.

They were headed away from us, but before we left them, they told us of a deer camp about twenty miles ahead on our trail and so, cheered by the thought of company for the night, we pushed on, determined to cover the twenty miles before we stopped. We reached the deer camp about eight that night.

Here we found five native houses and a small herd of two hundred fifty deer. They were southbound for the Chaun River where fish abound in the winter time. There are a number of these roving bands of natives who are not properly the deer men of the interior, for these latter are quite self-supporting and do not have to go about in search of food.

Like all of these roving bands, the one that we met that

night was extremely hospitable. Immediately the men unharnessed our dogs, chopped feed for us, and invited us into their houses. Seal oil was scarce and had to be conserved, so the inside of the house was quite dark. But our eyes became accustomed to it, and when the old lady in charge of the house passed us a wooden tray with something chopped up on it, we saw readily enough that it was food and the native host and I fished in. But Kavelin held back, feeling finicky about the food, and asked me what it was that I was eating. I told him that it was frozen salmon trout, and delicious. Later, I discovered that it was frozen deer meat; but frozen meat and frozen raw fish have very little flavor and unless you can see what you are eating, it is almost impossible to tell the difference.

The natives, both on the coast and in the interior, boil meat only once a day and eat it just before going to bed. This is probably because they have so little fuel and have to conserve it carefully. Years ago the natives in this part of the country had vast herds of deer, but hoof and mouth disease hit Siberia, ravishing the herds, and wolves have accounted for a good many others. Not that the natives let anything go to waste. If a deer has been killed by a wolf and any of it is left at all, they will eat what is left. Similarly, they will eat an animal that has died of disease. Now and then a brown bear will kill one of their herd and when this happens most of the carcass is usually left for the natives, for a bear likes his food partly digested. After killing a deer, he tears it open and devours the stomach. If the stomach is well filled, he usually lies down and takes a nap. When he wakes he eats the head but will not touch the rest of the body unless he is extremely hungry. Sometimes a female who has cubs will throw the whole carcass across her back and pack it home with her, but usually it is left where it is killed, and the natives, finding it, take it home and eat it.

The camp in which we stayed was entirely out of tea and sugar and, although our own supply was running low, we gave them some of ours. It began to look as though we would soon run out of these commodities, although we left the ship with a very generous supply of them, for at every native camp we felt we had to leave a little something in expression of appreciation for their hospitality. This was not because any of them would have complained had we not done so, for as I have said many times, they are among the most genuinely hospitable people in the world; but if you have ever tried to eat, with a lot of hungry children standing around looking at you, you will know exactly how I felt surrounded by these natives. Even though I knew that it might work inconvenience or hardship on us later, it was impossible to refuse to share with them and keep any liking for myself.

We spent only one night at this camp and pushed on, with Kavelin's sled, as usual, bringing up the rear. The natives, meanwhile, took a leaf from his book, pulling their sleds in between his and mine so that, as usual, I was breaking trail. It began to ruin my disposition for, while I don't mind leading all the time in nice weather on a good trail, when one has to plow through deep snow and travel over gravel bars in the river, or face a howling gale constantly, or take the responsibility of losing one's way in the dark,

or of driving into an open spot in the river, and while working his head off at this, looks back constantly to see the
others comfortably seated on their sleds, it makes his blood
boil.

Also there is the point of view of the training of the dogs
to consider. If you stay continually behind another sled,
you will eventually ruin your team, for they get into the
habit of trailing, and when you try to go in the lead, they
will refuse to go. The only way to keep the dogs in the
proper frame of mind is to take turns in leading, and that's
the only way, also, for men to keep in condition, so that the
driver of the lead team gives his legs some exercise. I always
made it an unbreakable rule never to stop my dogs behind
another team, but, if I was following, to drive at least
abreast of the leading team before stopping. But Kavelin
knew no consideration other than making things comfortable for himself and spending as little effort as possible.

Two days after leaving the native town Kom in Whats
parted with us, changing his direction and plan of travel as
spontaneously and easily as a roving fox might have. We
ran across an old deer trail and Kom in Whats suddenly decided that he was very hungry for deer meat, so, quite care-
free, he turned away from us and started to find the deer
men.

On that same day one of the native drivers' teams suffered
the loss of one of its members. We had just climbed a mountain and were going down the other side of it to get on to
the "Pala Wam" (Pala River) which flows into Chaun Bay.
On the descent we had hard, firm snow which carried us
along with the speed of an express train. The trail fol-

lowed along the edge of a precipitous snow bank which furnished a drop of twenty or thirty feet should we go over it. The dogs, for some reason tearing along in the exhilarating joy of speed, insisted upon staying at the very edge of the bank. No amount of yelling at them would make them budge an inch toward greater safety.

As usual, my sled was in the lead, and no matter how hard I pushed my brake stick down and held on to it, it was physically impossible to stop the sled. The snow was firm and smooth, but here and there under it was a large rock, and whenever the brake stick would hit one of these, I felt as though my arms and my leg, against which I braced it, were about to be pulled out. My shoulder sockets ached with pain and at every impact my head would come back with a snap. Even now, after all these years, I can feel the kink it produced in my neck. My leg felt as though it had been hit with a ten-pound sledge. It hurt so that I soon gave up my original impulse to shout and swear and felt like crying with pain and the sense of futility. When we finally stopped at the bottom, I was so angry and in such pain, that impulsively and without thinking, I strode forward to beat the dogs. But they looked up at me so happily, their tails wagging and their eyes shining with the joy of the run they had just had, that as always happens, my arm dropped helplessly and I could do nothing about it.

One of the native drivers, however, used his brake stick freely and hit one of the dogs too hard on the head, as a result of which we had to shoot him.

Three days later, at ten o'clock in the morning, we sighted a deer camp consisting of two houses, and went up to it. Here we found a native who said his name was "Omrilkan," rather a wealthy deer man with a beautiful herd of two thousand head. He greeted us and then, without asking us any questions, walked away, drove his entire herd up to the camp, lassoed two deer and, taking out his sticking knife, quickly struck each deer behind the right front leg. The animals looked rather surprised and then, without a sound, their eyes glazing, dropped. Omrilkan took a little of the blood of each deer, and with a ritualistic gesture, sprinkled it to the four winds in propitiation of his gods; he then proceeded to skin and dress the deer. He knew that we would be out of dog feed on account of the continual storms, and although he had never seen us before, his instinctive hospitality immediately asserted itself and he proceeded to furnish us with that which he knew we needed most. Then he invited us into the house and as we were about to enter, he deftly began to knock the snow and frost out of our fur clothing, as well as his own, with a native whisk-broom, which was nothing more nor less than the ribs of a deer. It is amazing how deftly the natives use this implement. Traveling in driving snowstorms, one's furs become loaded with snow and frost and if this is allowed to stay in the clothing when it is taken into a warm room, wet clothes are soon the result. Consequently, every native has a bone whisk-broom about and in a few minutes can get most of the troublesome snow and frost out of his garments.

Our native drivers were so pleased with this hospitality that they did not want to proceed, but Kavelin, impatient and irritable, insisted upon getting on regardless of the fact that the wind was blowing a gale and that by the time the deer were dressed the afternoon would be well advanced. At this point Mishka, the Russian, joined the natives, and when Kavelin insisted that we go on, peeled his parkey off and wanted to fight. Kavelin stepped back and drew the huge revolver which he always carried about his waist, but I stepped between them and tried as well as I could to calm the tempers and soothe the jangled nerves of everybody.

Finally, about three o'clock in the afternoon, we started out, but working against the gale that was blowing, we made only about eight miles before we had to camp in the open for the night.

When we got up the next morning the wind was blowing harder than usual and everyone was in a perfectly ghastly humor. I tried for the first time really to lay down the law about leading, but the other drivers simply refused point-blank to lead and I, knowing that we had to get to Chaun Bay soon if we were going to be able to keep our dogs' strength up with proper feed, had to carry on. So we struggled along in silence, the wind blowing us in circles, the dogs falling all over themselves as they breasted it. As the afternoon wore on we found less and less brush along the river banks and less gravel in the river beds, two indications that we were nearing the sea, and although no one had much to say to anyone else, as we camped in the open once more that night we went to sleep feeling that things would be better in the morning.

The next day we left camp about nine o'clock still facing the same terrific gale, but about noon we began to find driftwood along the banks of the river. Two hours later we found a fish cache and the beginning of a stake trail across the ice, and knowing from these things that we were now coming close to Sukolov's camp, the tension was suddenly broken and we all began to feel fine and to treat each other like human beings again.

Sukolov was a Russian who had been a trader for years and who for some time had lived at Chaun. He had a fine two-room log house which he occupied with his wife, a daughter of eleven, his father, and a native "Kolimchanian." We pulled up to it at about three in the afternoon and it looked like a paradise to all of us. Our dogs, too, immediately fell upon a banquet of Dolly Varden trout which Sukolov set before them.

CHAPTER XVII

For three days we stayed at Sukolov's place, sleeping, eating, drinking tea, and giving our dogs a chance to recuperate after three weeks of grilling work on the trail. Coming from the freezing temperatures through which we had traveled and through which we had slept, Sukolov's house seemed as warm as an oven and it was easy to relax in it and bake one's bones. The logs of which it was made were tightly caulked with moss and each of the two rooms that composed it was heated by a stove made from a gasoline drum cut in half.

From here we sent back the dog teams that had come with us from Cape North. I wanted to send my own dogs back to the ship, but was unable to get another team there and so I had to make them go along at least as far as Kolyma. We knew we would face a difficult time on the next lap of the trip, for we would reach no other house within twelve days' traveling and so what time we were not resting we spent in getting dog feed and other supplies together. By the time we had arranged for as much as we could, we had over three hundred fifty pounds of frozen fish alone per sled for dog feed. My own sled was loaded with about seven hundred pounds, including my luggage, grub, and dog feed, and not including myself. Meanwhile, we settled down to the simple life at Sukolov's, drinking tea without sugar and eating meat without seasoning, for all of the people along the coast were out of these provisions which they were forced to import because the *Elisif,* which had been scheduled to bring them these things, had become fast in the ice. There was no bread and none of us in our party had tasted any since leaving the ship, nor was there any flour at Sukolov's from which bread could be made.

It is absurd how insistently one can desire so simple a thing as a piece of bread when it is denied him, even though he is being well fed with other things. I remember at Sukolov's place I kept thinking wistfully of some bread a native woman had once baked for me under similar circumstances. We had run out of grub on a trip and arrived at a native camp late in the evening. With their usual hospitality, the natives tried to do everything they could to make us comfortable. Early in the morning the daughter of the house, one of the filthiest human beings I have ever seen, brought out a wooden bowl, filled it with flour, put some baking powder and water in, and after the batter was thick enough, took it out and began to roll it into shape on her bare leg. Whenever she lifted the dough there would be a long dirty black streak on it where it had come in contact with her leg, and when she had finished with her rolling and kneading, that part of the leg was the one comparatively clean spot on her body. But so hungry was I for bread that I shall never forget how good the finished product tasted.

While we waited at Sukolov's, two dog teams arrived from Kolyma after twenty-one days on the trail, and reported very bad traveling. Four deer teams also arrived from the interior, driven by fine looking old natives dressed in their best winter furs and seemingly very prosperous and happy. The interior deer men have a social system which works out very well. From the time a native is six years old until he is thirty, he works hard and ceaselessly. After he is past the age of thirty he retires, leaving the younger persons to do all the work except taking care of the house, fixing sleds, and odd jobs like that. Consequently, about the time a man has reached his prime and is ready to enjoy life, he has the leisure in which to do it and has a very good time indeed.

The children herd the deer and proceed with a sense of responsibility and self-dependence that is magnificent. If they are caught in a storm they catch two deer, hobble their front legs, make them lie down back to back, crawl in between them and go to sleep there as snug as a bug in a rug.

I remember being laid up in a deer camp once for four days during one of the worst blizzards I have ever seen. During all of that time the ten-year-old son of the house was missing, out somewhere in the snow—just where his parents had no idea. But they showed absolutely no sign of concern. It never seemed to occur to them that there was anything to worry about. And sure enough, when the storm was over, the son came in a little hungry but quite unharmed. He had simply slept four days in the lee of a cliff, sheltered by the bodies of his herd.

The natives call all white men "Tan yen." They call Russians "Mel ye tan yen," which means match-men, because the early Russians first introduced matches. Americans they call "Pen owk wil len," which means the people who first brought them objects in oblong forms such as files, plug tobacco and so forth. They call the Lamoots "Karamkin" which means "land Chinamen."

After our three days' rest we left Chaun in the driving face of the blizzard and made thirty-five versts to the home of Mallcoff, a Kolimchanian trapper. Here I was pleased by the arrival of a Lamoot, who had come simply to pay his respects to me. This has happened several times along the trail and has always pleased me because I know it is the result of the years of fair trading I have done with the natives, and I find that I cherish their good opinion of me just as I do that of the men with whom I do business in America.

The Lamoots live to the south and west of the territory through which we were going and, like the Chuckchos among whom we were traveling, they have deer herds; but instead of driving them on sleds they ride them, using a primitive saddle, and since they are quite small and slight the deer carry them without much effort.

A Lamoot costume is one of the most picturesque in Siberia. I was so struck with it when first I saw it, that I immediately wanted a complete outfit. I finally succeeded in getting a woman's suit, consisting of a pair of long fur boots made like rubber hip boots with a strap attached to the belt. The coat reminded me of a Prince Albert and had lead washers around the bottom so that it would hang properly. The fur cap was shaped like a hood, beautifully made, and there was an apron made of deerskin at the bottom and buckskin at the top. The whole was beautifully decorated with beads. I looked it over and felt very proud. All I wanted was the pair of trousers to go with it. I told the Lamoots I wanted the whole outfit and asked for the trousers. At first they only smiled courteously, saying nothing, and for several days I tried to get the missing part of the outfit, without success, always getting only a smile which was courteous and yet showed that I was amusing them very much. Now and then I saw them gathered in groups, talking to each other and laughing quietly to themselves. Obviously, they were having some sort of friendly joke at my expense. When I asked them about it they grinned and said trousers were much too expensive, but when I persisted and said that it did not matter, they lapsed again into smiling silences. Finally, one day when one of the natives seemed to be unusually friendly, I asked him what the joke was, and grinning broadly, he told me they never wear any trousers.

As we proceeded on the trail toward Kolyma we began to pass countless deadfalls strung along the beach, made of driftwood and set and baited, waiting for white fox. While we were at Mallcoff's place he brought in sixteen white fox after a tour of inspection of only a part of his string of deadfalls. The year before he caught two hundred sixty-three in this manner.

Also we ran across the trail of the Roald Amundsen expedition that wintered at Ion Island at the mouth of Chaun Bay. All of the trappers whom we met spoke of him with the greatest affection, and when we told them of his death they were visibly saddened. One of the trappers showed us a watch which Amundsen had given him; another a shotgun. He was a veritable Santa Claus to them all. He gave them feed for their dogs, presents for themselves and their families, and would never, under any circumstances, take any remuneration from them.

Here we began to leave the country of the Chuckchos and enter that of the Yakuts. We sent our Chuckcho driver back and engaged one Yakut and one Kolimchanian to go with us as far as Kolyma. Meanwhile, the weather was variable, with a persistent tendency to be disagreeable. I remember hesitating one night before going in to sleep in the comfortable log house we were fortunate enough to find, because I wanted to stay out a while and enjoy the spectacular beauty of the northern lights. But finally I went in, pleased with the hope for fine weather in the morning. When I awoke in the morning such a terrific storm was raging that we had to stay for two days where we were.

When we pushed on again the weather was clear and cold. We expected to make camp on the bay in two days, but on the second day we apparently got off our course and traveled up mountains and down deep ravines until our dogs were completely exhausted and refused to proceed. Their feet had been breaking constantly through the crust on the snow and were in bad shape, and the front legs of one of my leaders was stripped of hair for a distance of three inches. Finally, worn out, hungry, and feeling the cold much more because of our lack of food, we camped without any wood to make a fire, crawled into our sleeping bags as we were and kept pounding our feet together in an attempt to keep them from freezing. I lay there thoroughly miserable and numb with the cold, my feet rhythmically pounding each other, and trying to go to sleep. This, of course, was impossible, for each time I began to lose consciousness, my feet would get so cold that I would wake up again and start pounding them once more.

Some of the natives have learned the trick of sleeping and keeping their feet going at the same time. I remember once at Anadir making a four-day trip with dogs and natives. There was with us a native athlete, a man whom I often saw carrying out systematic athletic exercises. He would run in a circle for hours. Part of the time he would carry a big rock over his shoulder in his right hand and run in one direction; then he would shift it to his left hand and run in the opposite direction. The first night we camped on this trip it was exceedingly cold and I got no sleep, so that I had the opportunity of watching this athlete. Instead of lying down in the snow, he sat up in the crotch of a willow about four feet high, just high enough to keep his feet off the ground. Immediately he began kicking his feet together and although he promptly fell into a sound sleep, and stayed asleep until morning, his feet kept knocking together in perfect rhythm all night long.

But none of us on this trip had learned that trick and so we spent a miserably unhappy night.

In the morning we had an awful time getting started. The dogs were physically exhausted and so were we, and our tempers were all on edge. We were at the bottom of a deep canyon and the dogs could not pull the sleds up the mountainside—so we had to double up, hauling the sleds up one at a time with twice the usual number of dogs on each sled. We had had no dinner the evening before and had not even had a cup of hot tea with which to start the new day. But at about eleven o'clock we arrived at the point we had intended to reach the night before, made some tea, cooked some deer meat, and adding a load of driftwood to our other supplies, we started off across country quite comfortable again.

It was difficult to know how fast or how far we were traveling, for distances in the Arctic are measured entirely by relative conditions. If you ask a native how far it is to a given place, he will say, "Suppose good dogs, close to; no good dogs, long ways."

For two days we traveled uneventfully, encountering a number of trappers' *povarnys* (little shelters in this part of the country usually built of logs), each containing a primitive stove. They were built by the trappers for shelter while they are minding their deadfalls, and they are a godsend to travelers in stormy weather.

On the third day, just as we were about to start from camp, our dogs suddenly went wild; leaving the trail, they plunged through the darkness over logs, cakes of ice and hummocks at a terrific speed. We thought that they had scented a fox or bear, but soon we saw the light of a small fire ahead and found two trappers about to make camp. It was a delight to us to find company, and we built an especially large fire and sat around it in a circle until late at night, swapping news. I was the only one in the whole group who had a watch (except Kavelin) and at regular intervals all through the evening someone would ask me what time it was, just for the innocent pleasure of seeing me take out my watch. This had become by now quite a nuisance on the trail, for not only Kavelin bothered me about it as he had from the beginning of the trip, but the natives also had come to enjoy the game, so that every hour or so someone would make me take off a glove, pull back a long fur cuff, light a match if it happened to be after dark, and see what time it was. But on this night it was so pleasant to be sitting sociably around the big fire that it didn't annoy me at all if someone asked the time.

The next night we camped with the last coast Chuckcho we were to see on the entire trip. He and his wife lived alone in a hut one hundred and fifty miles from their nearest neighbor. I asked him why he lived so far away from other natives and he told me simply that he liked a quiet and peaceful life without others around to bother him. I think that he was the poorest native in worldly goods that I ever saw in Siberia but he seemed, on the whole, contented and happy. He recounted how, during the winter before, he had gone twenty days without food, living on rawhide, old skin clothes and the like, but he did not seem to have minded it much.

We arrived at his house while it was still daylight, and since it was a fine day, I queried why he was not out hunting. He answered that there was no seal that day, so he had not gone out. When we had had tea, I discovered an old pack of playing cards lying beside the oil lamp. They were so completely worn out from handling that I couldn't tell the difference between a four of hearts and an eight spot. Then the native told me that the cards always told him what to do. He would lay them out three in a row until they were all out, and following some fortune-telling technique which I could not penetrate, he could discover from them whether he ought to go hunting. On nice days it seemed, more often than not, that the cards would say, "no seal." On stormy days, even if the cards said "seal," he could not go out. So usually he went hungry.

I saw a pile of two-foot iron bolts about five-eighths of an inch thick, and some other heavy iron bars, which apparently had been a part of some ship's hardware. I asked him about them and he said that a lot of wreckage had come ashore about a month before, with many fine planks which make good firewood, and that there had been the corpse of a white man wrapped in canvas that had drifted to shore on a cake of ice. Beyond that I could get no information, and to this day I haven't the slightest idea to what ship's crew belonged the poor devil who died on the ice.

Before we left the native's house the following morning, he demanded four fish, promising us fine traveling that day if we gave them to him, otherwise we would suffer a severe blizzard. I thought that three days of fine weather would be pleasanter than one, so I gave him twelve fish.

Two days later we arrived at Soharmi, a village of twenty houses with ice windows and earth piled on their ceilings for roofs. Each day the blocks of ice, which served as window glass, are scraped, which keeps them beautifully translucent. Ice windows keep the house much warmer than glass windows do.

By now Kavelin was paying for his inactivity with a badly frozen nose. My nose and those of the other two drivers were frost-bitten, too, but we had been so active, with jumping over the rough ice we had encountered during the last two days' traveling, and from righting the sleds which frequently upset, that in spite of the bitterly cold weather, we came out pretty well; but poor Kavelin was in agony. However, there was little that could be done for him.

Catch of fox at Kolyma, Siberia

We stayed only one night at Soharmi and then pushed on to Nizhni Kolymsk, the most important distributing point on the Kolyma River. It is here that steamers come and discharge their freight for redistribution to up-river villages by steam and gasoline launches operated by the Gostorg and Yakuttorg, the two government trading organizations. Owing to our inability to get this far in the *Elisif* to land supplies, we found a great shortage of foodstuffs and other supplies here.

We decided to stay over for a couple of days to find fresh dog teams, and I enjoyed myself in making a superficial inspection of the furs which had been collected the preceding year and which were waiting until such time as we could get in for them with the ship. At this one place alone I found the following collection held by the Gostorg and Yakuttorg:

```
83265  squirrel
26737  ermine
  715  red fox
   21  cross fox
    1  silver fox
 7769  white fox
    2  blue fox
    1  otter
  378  laskey
   22  wolverine
  800  reindeer fawn
   25  wolf
   39  pood 30 lbs. mammoth ivory
  25#  walrus ivory
```

There was nothing to do but wait. I looked around for something of interest to buy and take back with me, such as an old samovar, but could find nothing, and that reminded me of an experience I had had in buying samovars once before.

It was during my early years in Kamchatka. As I left in the fall, I asked a Chinese who was there to try to get me ten or fifteen old copper samovars. When I returned the next spring he came to me with great delight, saying that he had found them and would bring them aboard the next day. I was pleased, too, and looked forward expectantly to see his collection. I was amazed the next day when I saw him come aboard with a sack on his shoulder, in which I thought there could not possibly be room for ten or fifteen samovars of any size. I was mistaken. Dropping the sack to the deck, he picked it up by the bottom, opened it, and dumped onto the deck what had been fifteen beautiful samovars, all of them smashed flat with a hammer! He had no idea that I wanted them as antiques, but thought I was buying junk and had done me the favor of making the old copper easier for me to carry.

Finally we left Nizhni Kolymsk and found clear, stimulating weather with little wind. It did not seem particularly cold, though the temperature was actually fifty degrees below zero (Fahrenheit). By four o'clock we arrived at Kimkina and stayed with a former trader named Soloveov, who had a fine log house with three large rooms, high ceilings and beautifully cared for ice windows. Here, as with the natives, rich or poor, we were shown marvelous hospitality, without a thought of payment. I don't suppose there is another place in the world where a traveler can go so far and be fed and housed by strangers without paying anything for it. At Soloveov's house Kavelin and I even slept in a bed with a spring. To be sure, there was no mattress, but we had a fine thick brown bearskin in its place. And before we went to bed we ate a regal meal consisting of dried fish, fish balls and frozen cream or "hiyak."

When it is served, hiyak looks like taffy. The cream is placed in deep plates to freeze solid and afterwards is broken in pieces and placed on the table.

Our hostess did not join us at supper but sat at a side table, with a large samovar at her elbow, completely silent and quite motionless, save when she was refilling our glasses with tea.

We had invited a native in to have tea with us, and through my lack of knowledge, I inadvertently insulted him. There was a sugar bowl with a glass top on the table. I helped myself to the sugar and replaced the top. The native said nothing but immediately got up and left. Later I learned that when you invite anyone to tea you must be sure to keep the cover off the sugar bowl, or else he will misinterpret this fact to mean your refusal to allow him to have sugar.

The next day I retreated from my insistence on walking and began traveling as a passenger on one of the sleds. Both Kavelin and I were both rather worn out by now and were getting rather thin. The wrinkle of fat which I had been wearing around my waist for months had entirely disappeared. In this kind of traveling in the Arctic you can count on losing at least a pound a day until you are down to bone and muscle.

But I found that although a day's riding rested me considerably I was far too cold for comfort as a passenger. After that respite and a night spent in a one-room log cabin about fourteen by sixteen, which contained, in addition to ourselves, six adults and five children, I started out the next day running beside the dogs as I had before. Kavelin, who by now was perishing from the cold, still could not be moved. He put on all the clothes that he had, and in addition, wriggled himself into his wolfskin sleeping bag and lay on the sled suffering pitifully. At tea-time we stopped at an "Ukager" house.

A century ago the Ukagers were the principal tribe in the Kolyma district, but some disease (apparently smallpox) has practically wiped them out, so that now there are scarcely one hundred and fifty families left. They tell of epidemics so severe that they could not bury the dead and were forced to put the bodies in the same cellars which they used for fish storage.

After tea we went on, arriving at about nine P.M. at our first typical "Yakut" house. The Yakuts are more or less Russianized and their houses, which are made of wood, have a peculiar shape like that of a short boat with a very broad beam. Heating and cooking depend on a fireplace made from poles plastered with mud. Live coals are raked out onto the hearthstone and placed under the cooking pots. Incidentally, the wood is placed perpendicularly on the fire instead of horizontally. This gives a greater draft and is less apt to make smoke. As soon as a guest arrives, even before a word of greeting is spoken, new wood is placed on the fire. This constitutes a ritualistic gesture of welcome, and a very pretty one it is, as well as being very significant to anybody who has spent long cold hours on the trail.

The interior of one of these houses looks like a ship's forecastle. Permanent bunks are built in a connecting chain all around the sides. These serve as seats during the day and as beds at night. There are no chairs. It is almost impossible to see the ceiling, since drying racks for footgear and clothing, and sack-like hammocks hung from the ceiling to hold the babies, completely obscure the view. In this first house in which we stayed, which was about twenty by twenty-six, I counted twenty-two persons, not including several babies which hung from the ceiling and which I didn't bother to count.

The next day I discovered one of the reasons why reports of distances given us by different natives vary so much. Some of them calculate distance by "sabachi," the long, or dog verst, and some by "kony," the short, or horse verst.

On December fourth, after six weeks of traveling, we arrived at Sredne-Kolymsk, where Kavelin lived, and I spent the night at his home.

This is as good a place as any to tell of something which it is a little difficult to discuss without offense, yet which seems to me to be interesting enough to report. I have often been asked what happened on the trail when one had to answer a call of nature with no conveniences of any kind within miles and the temperature often fifty or sixty degrees below zero. There is also an additional difficulty which the man who has not traveled with Arctic sled dogs does not realize. These dogs, which are kept half starved most of the time in order to keep them in good working condition and who will eat practically anything, constitute a very real danger to a man who is evacuating his bowels in the open, surrounded by them. The traveler with dogs has to adopt a definite method of protecting himself. First, it is necessary to find a place where a cliff or a large cake of ice offers protection from the back, so that you can constantly face the sled dogs. Then it is necessary to have a club or your brake stick or something of the kind and keep it swinging in front of you, driving the dogs off all the time that you are there, for they would not wait until you had left to begin their scavenging, and in their eagerness would as like as not take a piece of your flesh along. Add this hazard to the tremendous discomfort of baring your skin to a temperature sixty degrees below zero, and of getting your clothing full of snow, and you can see that a tremendous amount of courage may sometimes be necessary for a natural function which is taken as a matter of course in ordinary life.

The reason for mentioning this is that when we got to Sredne-Kolymsk, Kavelin confessed that since we had left the ship he had not once summoned up this much courage. It sounds incredible and I wonder to this day why the man did not die, but I also understood more clearly why he had been so difficult on the trip.

CHAPTER XVIII

THE next day I was pleased to have a visit from Jimmy Crooks, an Irishman whom we had left at Sredne the year before; he was to take the schooner *Nome* to Indigirka. It was the first time that a schooner had ever attempted the Indigirka River and Jimmy had had a terrible time taking her up there and bringing her back to Kolyma, but he made it, and had a great deal to tell me about the people with whom he had become acquainted.

For instance, there were the inhabitants of an old settlement that Russians call "Russky Ust." For nearly three hundred years they have lived entirely cut off from the outside world. The people are honest to a fault and take offense at the slightest act which might intimate a suspicion of their honesty. One of Jimmy's crew, for instance, got a little shack to live in and put a padlock on the door. From that day until the time he left not a single member of the settlement would enter his house or permit him to enter theirs.

The people live exclusively on wild reindeer and fish. The reindeer are killed with a spear or knife when they are swimming in the river. The meat is then buried in the ground until needed. Of course it becomes putrid, but decayed meat or fish does not seem to adversely affect their health. Nevertheless, most of them are in pitiful shape from lack of medical attention. Trichoma, leprosy, and venereal diseases are prevalent and add their toll to the ravages of poverty.

The women do all the work, cutting wood, caring for the house—even fishing—while the men hunt deer.

Jimmy had a cat on board ship and brought it ashore with him. No one in the village had ever before seen such a strange animal and they were terribly frightened. When he tried to bring his pet into one of the houses, the occupants made a mad scramble for the door. When the cat saw a dog and, arching its back, began to hiss and spit, the natives rushed to the dogs to protect them, thinking that they would all be killed. Jimmy gradually reassured them and finally encouraged one of them to stroke the cat; she began to purr and show other signs of affection, and this pleased these simple, childlike people, who eventually became very fond of Jimmy's pet, at times showing it a strange reverence, almost as though it were sacred and had some divine significance. Later, when it died, they wept openly and seemed to regard its death as a public calamity.

Jimmy was full of similar stories. He told, for instance, how he had taken the ship's stove ashore and set it up in his cabin. None of the natives had ever seen a stove before and they crowded in from all over the village to examine it in every detail. While this public exhibition was in progress, Jimmy went back to the ship for something. When he returned he saw smoke coming from the door of his cabin. Breaking into a run, he arrived to find smoke pouring, not from the top of the stove, but from the front, and the natives looking on in disgust, remarking that this new-fangled thing was no good. They had built a fire in the oven and closed the door.

He gave them little gifts, which were luxuries to them. To one woman he gave a pound of cocoa. The next evening she asked him to come over and share it with her. When he arrived he found that she had dumped the whole pound into a stew made of rotten meat. After one taste, Jimmy managed to beg off, but the natives thought the cocoa made the stew delicious.

To another woman he gave a pair of shoes. Several weeks later he saw her hobbling about in them as though her feet were in great pain, but she was smiling delightedly and displaying them to everyone she met. Looking closely at her feet, he saw that she had the left foot in the right shoe, and the right in the left. When he pointed this out to her she merely replied that she thought they looked much finer if the toes turned out instead of in.

These people seemed pleased with their isolation, and even proud of it. Like the lonely native I had met who guided his life by fortune-telling cards and lived a hundred and fifty miles from his nearest neighbor, they apparently do not want closer communication with anyone. Some of them do not even know their own names, but no one cares. They even seem afraid that their dead may join the rest of the world, for as soon as one of their number dies they cut the sinews in his legs, to make it impossible for him to walk away. When Jimmy finally lifted the schooner's anchor and left them, they all crossed themselves, wishing him God-speed, but apparently hoping that the schooner would never return.

The wild deer, of which there were many along the river,

were less shy than the people. Never having seen a large boat before, they were absolutely unafraid of it; driven by curiosity, they would come out into the river to get a better look at it. One herd swam alongside for some distance, so close that one of the men on board killed eleven of them with his sheath-knife, without even frightening the others away. Jimmy pulled one of the young ones on deck by catching hold of its horns. He kept it on board for a week, then he put it over the side; but it kept swimming alongside the boat, trying to climb aboard again. Several times they put it on shore, but it always returned to the ship. Finally, they took it on board again, as the only solution to what was becoming a nuisance.

We left Sredne over an old government trail which the Tsar had had cut through timber over two hundred years ago for the transportation of passengers and supplies between Yakutsk and Sredne, a total distance of 2,500 versts. Sredne-Kolymsk was then a penal colony and all prisoners were taken over this trail. Sometimes it took them two years to get from St. Petersburg to prison, driven along by the whips of their guards. Obviously, many of them never got there alive, and many others died on the way back after they had served their terms or had procured pardons through the intercession of friends.

The country here was as flat as a pancake and dotted with hundreds of lakes connected by an intricate network of rivers. Between the lakes the trail ran through the forest. In many places it was not over three feet wide and the branches of the trees at either side touched each other above us, their burdens of frost and snow gleaming in the sunlight like polished silver. Now and then we would meet other caravans, sometimes horse-drawn, sometimes using reindeer, with the drivers riding on the animals instead of on the sleds. The Yakuts always travel this way, piling their baggage as well as themselves on their horses' backs, even though the sleds behind them are empty. But the horses are chunky, strong looking animals and are kept in good shape. They do not seem to mind their loads.

During this stage of the journey I had a "zemchik" (driver) who added a weird and frightening note to the caravan. He wore on his head a hood made from the head of a wolf with the ears sticking straight up. The poor fellow was also crippled and a hunchback, which gave him a limping, shuffling walk and a stooped position. At night he would go ahead looking for the trail and when he returned, shuffling along toward us in the half light, his body bowed and with the fearsome looking wolf's head coming at me, I was sometimes so startled that I was close to the point of shooting.

When two other traders joined our caravan we looked like a circus; five dog teams, two men on horseback, and four reindeer teams, all traveling together, led by my hunch-backed zemchik with his wolf's head.

Every day we encountered a family or an individual who would make an excellent story. One day we had tea at a house thirty miles removed from its nearest neighbor, occupied solely by an old lady who was entirely dependent upon herself. She cut her own wood, caught her own fish, cut and hauled the hay, and did everything necessary to sustain her own life and that of her animals.

The next night we stopped with a prosperous Yakut family, where we found a member of a Russian scientific expedition connected with the Department of Fisheries, and we spent the evening talking about the gold strike at Simchan. We got very little sleep in this house for one of the old men snored like a pig all night long, and one of the children cried incessantly through the entire night. It was obviously a cry of pain that came from the child, so in the morning I looked it over to see if I could find out what was wrong with it. I found a huge burn on one of its heels; apparently the poor youngster had stepped on a live coal which had fallen out onto the hearthstone. I put some vaseline on it, bound it up, and he seemed to feel a little more cheerful about it. We stopped twenty-four hours in this house and all day long people kept coming and going as though we were in a jolly sort of roadhouse. A Russian with two Yakuts arrived from Yakutsk. They had been three months on the road—a journey which I had expected to make, going in the other direction, in twenty-five days. They reported that the "trackt" (trail) would not be established for some time.

Establishing the "trackt" is a yearly custom on this trail. Over a distance of forty or sixty versts men are stationed with deer or horses, and are kept in readiness to leave on short notice with the mail or passengers; but that year there was some kind of labor dispute which had delayed arrangements.

I also learned from these Russians that my old friend, the *Polar Bear*, which Captain Lane had used during the search for Stefansson, was at Yakutsk. Chris Gudmansen had brought the *Polar Bear* to Kolyma but had taken her so far inland on high water that as the tide went out she was grounded and he had been forced to abandon her. For three years she stayed high and dry on the beach. Then a group of clever Kolimchanians dug a canal from the river to the boat and floated her successfully.

When we arrived at Sulgutter, we met one of the agents of the Dalgostorg and began at once to negotiate with him for reindeer, for from here on we would have to travel by reindeer teams and horses. Before we reached Sulgutter I asked my zemchik how large a place it was and he enthusiastically told me that there were plenty of houses there. When I asked him to be a little more explicit, he paused thoughtfully for a little while and told me that there were four.

We managed to pick the best of the four, inhabited by a man named Vassily. Like most of the native Yakut homes, it was a religious household. In one corner of the single room which made up the house, there were twelve icons, before which the inhabitants crossed themselves when entering the house and after eating. Vassily had one luxury which is seldom found in a Yakut house—a lamp. I showed him my flashlight and he was very much interested in it, but, unfortunately, I was unable to demonstrate it to him for the battery had become exhausted and would no longer light. This seemed to worry him, and later in the evening he went out, coming back with a small can of kerosene from which he solemnly tried to fill my flashlight.

Our arrival at a Yakut shack was always an interesting occurrence. Usually, before we were very close to it, one of their dogs would bark a warning, which would be followed by women and children who poured out of the house to stare at us as we drove up. All went well until I would get up from the sled, when the whole crowd usually made a bee-line toward the door of the shack, as if they had seen the devil himself. I am a large man and my fur clothing must have made me seem huge indeed. Perhaps that is what scared them, or perhaps there was something else foreign-looking about the whole outfit; I never discovered what it was, but there was no question that they were always badly upset. Once I got inside the house and threw off my outer clothing, they tamed down and became extremely friendly and hospitable. The women (unlike the Chuckchos) would wash their hands, throw wood on the fire, and begin polishing up the cups and saucers for tea. The children, having crawled behind whatever they could find to shelter them, would peer out from their hiding places with bright eyes, like mice, ready for a quick getaway; but they were quickly won by a bit of candy and soon would be hanging to me like a lot of kittens.

I always had difficulty getting through the doors of these shacks, which were only about twenty-two inches wide, four and a half feet high, and slanted inward at an angle of about forty-five degrees. At first I tried to go straight in but invariably I got stuck; when I tried to force my way, I usually had to be pulled out; or, if I went through with a rush, I landed in a heap in the middle of the room. The first time I did this, the household was charmed, believing this to be the American form of salutation to a host. Later, I developed a definite technique; approaching the door backward,

I would put one of my legs through, then, backing up a little, put the other one through; bent almost double, I backed up some more and finally straightened up safely inside.

Having entered, it is the custom to shake hands with everybody and say "Dorova," meaning "be healthy." On leaving, the handshaking is repeated with the farewell "Prashai." Everybody in the household lines up for the handshaking, like a lot of bellhops in a Japanese hotel. They enjoy this so much that frequently some members of the household will shake hands with you at one end of the line and run around in back to reach the other end of the line, so they can shake hands again. One morning, just for fun, I counted, and found that I had shaken hands twelve times, although there were only seven persons in the room.

Here we parted with our dogs and I, who had never thought of myself as a sentimentalist, found that I was moved by a painful sense of loss. For forty-six days they had shared with me the bitter cold, hunger, and the painful traveling over a rough and hazardous trail. They had come through faithfully, always giving me the best they had in them. They were thin, worn down, and tired, but their eyes shone with loyalty as they looked up in answer to my voice. Looking at them for the last time, I suddenly realized that I loved them, and without caring who was watching or what anyone thought about it, I got down on my knees and, putting my arms around each of one, held him close to me as I told him good-by.

CHAPTER XIX

We started out again with the deer team in bad condition because of a forced trip they had just made in transporting some soldiers. It had been their first trip so they were fat and not in good trim. Ordinarily, they would have taken the first few days slowly, but the soldiers, who were in a hurry, drove the deer to the limit of their ability and exhausted them, obliging us to proceed much more slowly than usual.

It was a prosperous cattle country through which we drove, but the animals were not like those which you see in the United States. They looked like a cross between an American buffalo and a cow. The low temperatures (it is often as cold as sixty degrees below zero, Fahrenheit) did not seem to bother them a bit and all the cattle I saw there were in fine condition.

I asked an old man if the native Yakuts had always raised cows in this district. At first he said yes and then, after thinking about it a while, he told me a tale of the beginning of their herds, a tale which had been passed along to him by his grandfather.

Generations ago, he said, they had had their own Yakut Tsar, who ruled at Yakutsk. At that time they were harried by the Russians, and when some of the natives were cut off from Yakutsk by a band of Cossacks, they decided to travel as far to the east as possible, in an attempt to escape the continual trouble which the marauding Russians brought upon

Two Chukcho dressmakers from a nomad deer raising tribe. Note the
mastodon tusks

them. They had three head of cattle and one dog and with these they proceeded eastward for weeks until they came to the high range of mountains near the Aldon River. They gazed in awe at what seemed to them an impassable barrier, for looking up, they could see that the earth met the sky.

Discouraged, half-starved and worn out, they made camp and considered what to do next. Finally, they decided to return, even though they had to face the Cossacks again, for when the land met the sky, was it not conclusive proof that they had come to the end of the earth? But the day before they were ready to start on the back trail, they saw their dog go up the mountain and disappear in the clouds. They had no doubt but that he was gone forever but waited a little while to see if by any chance, he might return.

Sure enough, the next morning he came back; overjoyed, they came to the conclusion that if the dog could go to the sky, so could they. Shouting with pleasure, and buoyed up with new courage, they ascended into the clouds.

Soon, of course, they were on the other side of the range and here they found such fine grazing and such an abundance of game that they settled down to stay. The old man told me that all of the herds of cattle which the Yakuts now had in this district, came from the three head they had brought with them, which flourished and prospered and increased on the fine grazing lands in the valley to which they had dared to come.

The next morning, December sixteenth, I celebrated my birthday by shaking hands with myself, saying "Many happy returns of the day," and by drinking a cup of tea with the old man who had told me the story of the Yakut cattle. All this happened at four o'clock in the morning, which is approximately the time when most Yakut families rise—for what reason I haven't the slightest idea. None of them carry watches and they proceed more or less by instinct to regulate the hours of their meals. Usually they are up at four and begin the day with tea. About seven they eat a breakfast of frozen raw fish. Around ten they have dinner. At two they have tea and hiyak. And four hours later, at six, they have a supper of boiled fish. Any time after that is bedtime. In December, the days are so short that there are scarcely three hours of daylight, but even though they have no sun by which to tell the time, their eating habits are fairly regular. Although they have no timepieces, they do have a calendar of their own devising and making. It looks very much like a cribbage board, with holes for the months running up and down the board, and holes for the days running across. Each morning a wooden peg is moved forward one hole.

Like the Chuckchos, the Yakuts are very fond of tea, drinking innumerable cups of it. Also, like the Chuckchos, when a man has had enough he turns his cup upside down. Sometimes I forgot to do this and as a result had to drink one cup of tea more than I wanted, for once it had been poured it would have been the height of rudeness not to drink it. On this part of my trip my sugar supply held out well, for the Dalgostorg had given me granulated sugar which the Yakuts refused to use. They prefer hard loaf sugar from which they can bite off a piece, hold it in their mouths, and sip their tea through it.

They are a jolly, happy race of people. Though they have absolutely nothing which resembles luxury and no amusements save those which they seem to find in their own thoughts or in friendly intercourse with each other, a crowd of them together are constantly joking, singing, shouting, laughing, having the best time in the world. Physical discomfort seems to mean nothing to them. They sleep on beds made with small logs laid crosswise, like a corduroy road, with every one of them pressing into your body as you try to sleep. With the temperature in winter around fifty-five or sixty degrees below zero (Fahrenheit), they handle their fishnets through the ice with great dexterity. I saw one fellow, whose hands were getting stiff from this exercise, plunge them both into the icy water in order to restore circulation, and a moment later go on with his work as if nothing had happened.

Frequently along the trail we ran into a "samma strekla" (self-shooter), the hunting device used by the natives in this district with which to shoot deer. It consists of a large bow and an iron-tipped arrow, set against a tree at the right height. There is a trigger on it and a string attached to it which is stretched across a deer path, so that when the animal runs into it, the arrow is discharged and if it is properly set, the deer is killed. Obsolete rifles are used in the same manner. We were told that throughout this part of the trail the woods were full of these self-shooters and that traveling in the dark was extremely hazardous on account of them. For the same reason, when we camped at night, our deer would be tied up instead of allowed to run loose.

A great deal of our trail now was very difficult—uphill,

and down precipitous slides. Going up the mountain was all right, the deer taking the up-trail in their stride without apparent effort, but going downhill was a constant succession of hair-raising thrills.

The Yakuts hitched their deer to the sleds with a single leather strap. At each end of the strap there is a large loop. One loop is slipped over the horns and under the inside front leg of one of the deer, and the strap is then passed back through the bow of the sled, the loop at the other end being passed forward again under the inside front leg and over the horns of the second deer. When traveling, the strap keeps seesawing back and forth. If one deer is a few inches ahead of the other in the team, the one which is behind is continually hit by the sled until he gets tired of it and makes an extra long, fast jump, when the strap evens up with a jerk.

Going downhill, the deer simply jump to the sides to prevent the sled from running them down, and the sled rushes on ahead with the deer alongside, going like the wind, until the whole outfit comes up against a tree or is hurled into the deep snow. If a decline is too steep, the drivers stop at the top and hitch the deer behind the sled, so that the animals can hold it back to some extent.

We crossed the Indigirka River at Zachiversk, where I got a new zemchik, the best I had had so far. Mile after mile he kept his deer on the move and our trips downhill were like continuous roller-coaster rides. He would let his animals go at top speed, so that the sleds seemed off the ground most of the time as they darted from hummock to hummock. These deer had exceptionally fine large antlers which kept striking trees as we went along, and every time they struck one a bushel of snow would come down on top of me.

On Christmas Eve we arrived at Abbi, but there was no sign of Christmas about. Abbi is a rather imposing village in comparison with those through which we passed. We found about thirty houses and a church standing at the edge of a large lake, but in none of them was there any sign that it was Christmas Eve. How could there be when no one had anything with which to celebrate?

All along the trail, before coming in, I had been thinking of how perfect was the setting for a Christmas Eve celebration. There were millions of Christmas trees decorated by Nature with snow and frost in a glorious display such as no man could produce, lit by a bright full moon which would have made candles seem superfluous. Even the chimneys of the houses were made for Santa Claus. Their tops were only about ten feet above the floor and they were so large that one could drop through them easily without even getting sooty, and inside were racks full of fur socks and boots into which presents could be slipped. But no one had any gifts for anyone else, save the bare necessities of existence which they share freely.

I had with me a little loaf-sugar and about two pounds of mixed hard candy which I had got from a trader. With this I played Santa to the children all along the trail. It was pathetic to see how happy just a little candy made these youngsters. If I gave one of them a piece of candy or a piece of loaf-sugar, he would nibble at it just the least bit and then scuttle off into a corner to hide it for later consumption.

Looking at these kindly, hospitable, half-starving people, I longed to be a real Santa Claus to them. In Abbi at that time there was not a bit of tea, kerosene, or sugar, or any of a dozen common items which we regard as absolute necessities and take as a matter of course. They had fish and meat, and a few had cows so that they could have milk, but beyond that they had absolutely nothing.

The next morning, Christmas Day, I got up with a feeling of depression, which I suppose was really homesickness. The house was so dark, with only the dim light of the fireplace, that it was difficult to see one's way around and that made matters more gloomy. After a while I dug out one of the only two candles left in our equipment and lit it as a symbol of Christmas. Then I felt better.

Two days later we met the mail coming in from Yakutsk. The young man in charge of it stopped to ask us all the news. His home was at Sredne and he was so anxious to hear about everything that had been happening there that it was practically impossible to get any information from him in return. He wanted to know if his family had found the lost horse, how the cow was, but most of all he was curious as to whether or not his father had yet succeeded in selling the accordion.

The next night we camped at a *povarny* with a Yakut whom we had met going in the same direction as we were. Neither he nor we had much wood, so we made one fire, putting together what meat we had and cooking it in the same pot. My zemchik had a little beef which he put in, my interpreter some caribou meat, I put in some reindeer meat, and the Yakut some horse meat. It really was very good when it was all stewed up, and we had a fine time sitting around in a circle fishing bits of meat out of the pot while exchanging gossip.

For three days after our meal of beef, caribou, reindeer and horse meat, I find that I made no entry in my diary, save the distance, and on one day I neglected even to enter that. The trouble was a terrible, griping pain which doubled me up with such agony that I had to spend most of my time lying, as well as I could, on the sled. I think probably it was a touch of appendicitis, but since there were neither doctors nor hospitals about, I had only the pain to bear and was spared the additional burden of a doctor's diagnosis. Meanwhile, we were going through the most beautiful stretch of our entire trip. It was over a magnificent range of mountains, across spectacularly beautiful glaciers, and through canyons which made pale, in comparison, anything similar I had ever seen. The entire region abounded in game. Every day we saw herds of wild deer, some of them containing thirty-five or forty animals, and bands of mountain sheep. Both the sheep and the deer were very inquisitive and would run away only a few yards and then stop dead to look back at us.

It was on this part of the trip that I encountered a "yurta" (native house), which had running water, even though it had no plumbing. A large cone of snow was hung next to the fireplace over a bucket. The heat kept the snow melting slowly so that a gentle, steady stream of water kept dripping into the bucket. Two curved sticks ran down to the apex of the cone and were fastened together at top and bottom by rawhide straps. Ice could not be used this way as it would melt rapidly where the sticks touched it and fall out, but snow melts gradually and stays in its cradle until the last of it has dripped away in water at the bottom.

In this district cows were kept in a barn built actually as a part of the house, with an open door connecting the stable and the living room. Whenever the cows felt cold or perhaps merely sociable, they simply wandered in and stood or laid down before the fireplace.

As I entered the *yurta* I was conscious of the warm, moist smell of a cow stable. If the cows happened to be in the adjoining room, I could feel a warm current of air coming through the stable door. It made me wonder whether the cows were stabled thus for their own comfort or to furnish a heating plant for the family.

In one *yurta* where we had tea, an old lady, who was partially crippled, sat in a corner next to a cow which was eating from a manger built into the living room. Whenever the old woman wanted to get up, she leaned over, took hold of the cow's tail and pulled herself to her feet, and the cow took it as a matter of course.

On January sixth we arrived at Verkhoiansk, which is known to meteorologists as the coldest spot on earth. The record temperature there is ninety-two degrees below zero, Fahrenheit. When we reached it the weather was comparatively mild, as the thermometer only showed sixty-nine below.

As we approached the village all we could see was a pall of smoke hanging over the town, making it look like a manufacturing center, but it was only smoke from the chimneys of the houses. There was not a breath of wind and in the extreme cold the smoke hung close to the chimneys. The village consists of sixty-three log houses of various shapes and dimensions.

Here the local official asked me to take the mail to Yakutsk and I agreed to do so. It meant traveling night and day from then on, but it also meant greater co-operation in getting deer teams and general speeding up all along the way. From there we changed deer at each station and made as good time as possible.

On January tenth the sun "came back," like a great ball of fire over the horizon, and even though it gave us no heat, it was a lot of satisfaction to know that it promised warmth later on. All through this country the sun (which disappears the latter part of November, not to re-appear again until January) is referred to much more often in mentioning time than are the months of the calendar. If you ask anyone when he is going to start a trip, he will invariably tell you the time as a day or a week or a month "after the sun comes back."

With the return of the sun we got a new zemchik, a man who must have been well past seventy and who was half blind, but he seemed unconscious of his age or poor vision. During the entire trip we had no driver who handled his deer more recklessly on the trail. All day long he kept them at top speed. It was very dark and the blackness, combined with the steam which rose from the deer, made it impossible to see a thing.

For days we had been traveling uphill until finally we came to To-Ko-Lan Pass and suddenly there burst on our vision the most beautiful sight I have ever seen. The trail is only about thirty feet wide at the top of the Pass and we came upon it after days in which we had had scarcely any views at all. Suddenly it seemed as though the whole world were spread before us, and we were standing on the very top of it. The trail ahead looked almost as though it went straight down a sheer precipice.

At the very top there was a large cross on which our zemchik hung something, as if in propitiation before we started the descent. (Looking at the steep trail before us, I felt that if I had had my watch and chain handy, I would have hung them there, too.) Then he unstrapped the deer, lashed the sleds together and hitched all of the deer at the rear. I helped him push the sleds over the brink and stood in awe while the whole outfit, in a matter of seconds, took a drop of several hundred feet, the deer sitting on their haunches and sliding down after the sleds. I had a long pole which I jabbed into the snow as I followed them. I would take a couple of steps, hanging on to the pole, try to get a footing, move the pole forward and repeat. Finally we got to the spot at which the deer had found a landing place and were waiting for us. The zemchik was there long before I was and gave his deer a breathing spell until I caught up.

Then we started on the second lap. This time I went ahead. I was half way down to the next landing place when

I felt myself slipping. The only thing in sight was the mountain which I was trying in vain to hold onto and that terrible drop below me. Just as I knew I was gone, the sleds shot past me with the deer behind them and, frantically, as one of the deer brushed me, I threw my arms around his neck and hung on, my mind anxiously pleading with the animal to be good to me. The details of the next few seconds I knew nothing about. All I remember is that when we finally came to a stopping place, the deer and I stood up at the same time, looked each other in the eye in complete friendliness, and got ready for the next lap.

Here the zemchik put the two leaders in front of the sled and told me to get into my sled, for he saw two rocks right in the middle of the trail near the bottom, and felt that the only way the sleds could get around them was to have the deer in front, and enough speed so that they would automatically avoid the rocks and carry the sleds with them. We negotiated the trail nicely and finally stopped at the bottom, all in one piece, after the speediest ride I have ever had in any vehicle. Looking back up to the top, I blinked my eyes and had to pinch myself to believe that we had actually come down that precipitous descent. In a few minutes we had dropped a distance which would have taken us days to climb.

At the next station we changed our reindeer for horses, which were to be our motive power for the rest of the trip. They were quite a come-down from the picturesque animals which had hauled our sleds during the last lap of our trip, and very much slower.

With the acquisition of horses, we ran into increasing

evidences of civilization and with them came a diminishing interest in the trip, so far as I was concerned. I had been living among people without education, without comfort, without any of the qualities which we call culture, and especially without dishonesty. Now, one by one, little things disappeared from our outfit—a pair of fur boots here, a pair of socks there—for, you see, the people into whose presence we were now coming had more of the benefits of civilization and had learned more of its lessons.

Soon we came upon our first flour mill, consisting of two large, flat, disc-like stones about sixteen inches in diameter, with a hole in the top one, through which native rye and wheat was poured. When the top stone was turned, the grain gradually worked out between the edges of the stones as flour.

We also saw mothers feeding their babies out of proper, unbreakable nursing bottles made of small cows' horns, the tips of which had been cut off to allow milk and soft food to pass through. A mother would take some bread and meat, chew it for a while and then, taking a sip of milk into her mouth to mix the whole mess together, would spew it into the large end of the horn, while the child took the small end into its mouth and sucked.

By now I was half-exhausted as a result of the continuous traveling we had done since taking on the mail and by my absolute inability to fall asleep on a plunging, uncomfortable deer sled. For days I had been getting only an hour and a half or two hours of sleep in twenty-four; but an old zemchik whom we got at one of the stations understood my difficulty and found an exceptionally large sled for me on which he put a couple of armfuls of hay. He tucked me into my sleeping bag and I was unconscious in five minutes. But even then I did not sleep long, for one of the horses on the sled back of mine discovered the hay and every time he could get close enough, took a mouthful of it from my pillow. At first he only half waked me up, but when he made a quick grab for the hay and got hold of the hood of my parkey, pulling me half off the sled, I was wide awake. Then I lay in wait for him and the next time he tried it, I slapped him across the snout a few times with my hand. After that I got to sleep for a little while.

We arrived at Yakutsk on January sixteenth, where I celebrated with my zemchik and his mother over grilled steak and a bottle of port wine, after which I went to the hotel and had a glorious night's sleep. To be sure, it was a room which I shared with a Russian who was traveling to Moscow, but on that night I could have shared a room with a regiment of Russian soldiers and slept well.

I was held up at Yakutsk for four days, trying to get a visa on my passport. It seemed that I had been needing one for a long time and had actually made illegal entry into the Yakutsk Republic, but in all of the country through which I had passed there was never any place where I could get one and it never occurred to me to do anything about it.

The Yakutsk Republic has an interesting history. The entire province is twenty-nine times the size of Belgium and has a population of only two hundred and eighty thousand. The city of Yakutsk, the capital, was taken by a Russian Cossack named Yermak over three hundred years ago. When he arrived at Yakutsk he asked for permission to build on a piece of ground large enough to stretch a bull's hide over it. The Yakuts thought his request very modest and finally granted it. However, he did not spread the hide on the ground, as they had anticipated, but cut it into a long, very thin strip of rawhide which he stretched around enough territory to build for himself and his men a formidable fortress from which he ruled the Yakuts in the name of the Tsar of Russia. A part of the fortress is still standing.

Leaving Yakutsk, we pushed on to our last trip to Irkutsk. Time and again we met other vehicles, horses and sleds loaded with hay and other provisions. Every day brought increasing signs of civilization—houses and villages set more closely together, each with a little bath-house in which stones were heated to a white heat and which, when water was poured over them, made a thick cloud of steam for the kind of bath the Russians love.

Finally, toward the middle of February, we arrived at Irkutsk, the end of our journey, after four months of traveling over the most difficult trail I have ever followed. So far as anyone knows, no one had ever made the trip before, and I am not sure that even I would care to make it again. But, although I looked forward to a comfortable hotel room with bath, and felt like hailing with joy the sight of the Siberian Railroad which would take me out of Irkutsk, headed for home, I looked backward, too, with something like regret. For I was leaving behind me what were in many ways the finest and most satisfying adventures of my life.

CHAPTER XX

As soon as I got back to Seattle I outfitted the motor schooner *Nanuk*. I wanted to go back to Cape North and take supplies to the *Elisif* and bring out its cargo of furs along with those which had been collected for us since we left.

My daughter, Marion, then in high school in Seattle, had listened with fascinating interest to my stories of the forty-five-hundred-mile trip across Siberia from which I had just returned, and begged to go along with me. At first I was reluctant to take her, for although I had no expectation of getting frozen in again, one never knows what might happen, and there was the old superstition that a ship in the Arctic is not an ideal place for a woman. But she wanted so badly to go and was so self-reliant and eager, that I finally consented. We sailed on June fifteenth, loaded with supplies for both the Gostorg trading stations and the *Elisif*. Just as we were leaving, someone asked Marion if she was not afraid that the *Nanuk* might get stuck in the ice just as the *Elisif* had. I shall never forget her bright, excited smile as she answered.

"I hope we do get frozen in," she cried, "and have to make the trip out with dogs and reindeer as father did last winter. I'd love it."

I am not especially superstitious and I don't really think that that had anything to do with what happened, but later

I found myself wishing that Marion had not made that remark.

We got to the *Elisif* all right, meeting her on the very day when she finally broke free from the ice. Then the *Elisif*—under the Norwegian flag, with R. S. Pollister in command and Captain A. P. Jochimsen as ice-pilot—and the *Nanuk* with Marion and myself aboard, started for Kolyma. The *Nanuk* was a sturdy boat with a shallower draft than the *Elisif* and on account of this we were able to work the ice a little faster. Consequently, the two boats became separated and as the other boat tried to catch up with us, she ran into a heavy cake of ice with a long prong which projected under the water and it made a hole in her, five feet under the water line. Pollister reported to us by radio, but by then all we could do was to give him our position, since the ice was crowding in behind us so rapidly that we were unable to turn around and go to her assistance. Meanwhile, the *Elisif* was sinking rapidly and Pollister did the only thing that he could do—he beached her.

He left a couple of men in charge of the ship and with the rest of the crew he proceeded in launches and open boats along the coast and across to Nome, a distance of over 600 miles. Half-way across the Behring Strait they ran into a terrific storm, and though I have not the details, I know that the whole group was nearly lost; and when they finally got to Nome they felt sure that Providence had guided them there.

Meanwhile, we on the *Nanuk* reached Kolyma, discharged our cargo, and picked up one of the largest col-

Bill, Olaf Swenson, Pat Reid (Pilot), Marion and Capt. Milovzorov of the *Stavropol*

lections of furs which I had ever taken on in one season. Then we turned around and tried to accomplish what we had been unable to do when we got Pollister's distress message—go back. All the way along the coast we fought the ice until finally, when we got to Cape North, the ice fastened its grip on us and we were unable to move a foot. Just across the Cape, in almost the exact spot where the *Elisif* had spent the previous winter, was our old friend, the Russian steamer *Stavropol*, also fast in the ice.

Here we were, and so far Marion's wish had come true. We were frozen in so securely it was obvious that the ship would stay all winter, just as the *Elisif* had the winter before. But to Marion's proposal that we go out by dog sled over the route I had taken before I had to say "No." I would have been perfectly willing to take that trip again, and I think that I would not have hesitated to take Marion along, for she was an unusually able and fearless girl and had already shown that she was capable of standing the rigors of Arctic traveling. As a matter of fact, watching her conduct in the North, I could not help thinking how much better a traveling companion she would make on a trip like that than Kavelin. But there was another consideration. We had on board a cargo of furs with a market value of over a million dollars. The market was high just then—and there were very definite indications that before the winter was over it was going to break—so from a business point of view it was essential that we get our cargo out and on sale as quickly as possible.

Also, I wanted to get off as many of the crew of the *Nanuk* as I could. When a ship is wintering at a place like Cape North, the fewer people on board, the better they get along together.

So we got in touch by radio with the Alaskan Airways at Fairbanks, Alaska, and after considerable negotiations, arranged with them to transport our furs and our crew to Fairbanks by air at a cost of four dollars a pound for the furs, and seven hundred and fifty dollars each for the passengers.

Carl Ben Eielson, a pilot who had already won international fame for his flights in the Arctic—most notable of which was the one he had made with Sir George Hubert Wilkins from Point Barrow to Spitzbergen—was manager of the Alaskan Airways. He decided he would take charge of the job himself, and in October he and Frank Dorbandt made one trip to our ship, took out six members of the crew and as many of the furs as they had room for. After sizing up the situation, he decided that six trips would be necessary. Marion and I planned to stay on the ship until the last trip.

From that point on the story is one of tragedy. When Eielson made his first trip he had fine flying weather, and if he had been able then to do the whole job at a clip, there is little doubt that his mission would have been successful. But, meanwhile, another of the Alaskan Airways flyers was lost somewhere around Anchorage, and Eielson and Dorbandt both joined the search, while we waited with our furs on the *Nanuk*.

While we were waiting, the winter weather set in, with storms and blizzards which made flying more hazardous every day.

Finally, Eielson got in touch with us again, telling us the exact day he expected to arrive for the next load. He told us not to worry if he did not get there on the dot as he might be delayed for a day or two. The date planned was November ninth (1929).

Since Eielson himself had told us that he might not be able to make it on schedule, we did not worry when he failed to arrive—but we were all impatient to be off. Days drag slowly on a ship frozen in in the Arctic. Marion was having the time of her life—taking walks on the ice, talking with the crew, and, through an interpreter, with the natives, and reading all the books and magazines which we had brought along. But soon the temperature dropped to an average of fifty degrees below zero and there was a constant bitter north wind which made walking almost impossible. Marion was even reading our supply of books and magazines for the second time, so that she too was ready to leave. Consequently, when the second day brought no sign of Eielson, we all began to worry; on the eleventh of November, we learned by radio that Eielson and Earl Borland had actually taken off on the ninth, so we all knew that he must have been grounded somewhere between Fairbanks and Cape North. Whether he and Borland were alive or dead no one, of course, could know with any degree of assurance. Even if they were alive we knew that they were in hazardous straits, for undoubtedly they had not enough supplies to last them long, and in the bitter gale which was then blowing, the problem of shelter would be serious. We also knew that they would have difficulty in getting food for that year there was so much ice that we found it impossible to get enough seal or walrus to feed the dogs which we had aboard ship.

Soon reports began to come from the natives, which encouraged us. There was a story that Russian hunters had sighted an airplane west of Kolyntchin Bay on the ninth. The plane was said to have circled twice over their camp before disappearing toward the west. Another report came from a native near the same spot, who said that he had heard a plane which had apparently been seeking a landing place in the dark. According to this report, the roar of the motor continued for several minutes, stopped, started up again, this time louder than before, only to die out in ominous silence.

Newspapers, of course, at once published the fact that the two flyers were lost and the world waited in suspense while the search went on for them. Joe Crosson and Harold Gillam, old flying comrades of Eielson's, arrived in an Alaskan Airways plane and with them I flew over the district described by the Russian hunters and natives. It was difficult work and there were days on end when we could not move against the roaring fifty-mile-an-hour gale which swept Cape North. Meanwhile, our supplies were running low, especially the necessary gasoline; but the Soviet government had a small stock stored at Cape North and gave us permission to use it so long as it was replaced not later than January tenth, when the Soviet expedition, which was being formed for the purpose of searching for Eielson, would be ready to start operations.

Along with the Russian expedition. the Aviation Corporation of America also formed a searching party.

Occasionally new reports would come in, giving us hope that perhaps Eielson and Borland were still alive. There were several stories from natives of having seen smoke in the territory where the plane was supposed to have been grounded; but though we made several flights and dog sled trips into this locale, we found nothing. Our work was greatly hampered, of course, not only by the cold weather and the terrific blizzards, but by the fact that it had to be done during the time of year when darkness covers the Siberian coast for all but two or three hours a day. We all looked forward more eagerly than we ever had to the day when "the sun would come back."

The newspapers were interested, not only in the search for Eielson, but in the plight of our own party aboard the *Nanuk* with a shortage of supplies (which, as a matter of fact, never became serious for us). The fact that we had a seventeen-year-old girl aboard added greatly to their interest, of course. And the *New York Times*, getting in touch with us by radio, commissioned Marion to send a daily dispatch in regard to conditions and activities aboard ship as well as the progress of the search for Eielson and Borland, which, of course, centered around the *Nanuk*.

November and December passed and in spite of the many flights and trips by dog sled to visit deer camps and to search the country where the plane was thought to have been grounded, no sign of the flyers had yet been found.

One thing that the dog sleds did, however, was definitely to narrow the search, for at several deer camps and villages we found natives who told of having heard the plane—not only men, but old women and children who had been frightened by the sound, thinking it to be an evil spirit. They had hidden themselves in their huts, and gave us what were undoubtedly reliable reports, showing that Eielson had been set on his course. The search then continued with greater vigor than ever.

However, as the search narrowed, somehow or other our hopes that the two men might be alive increased. Finally, on the twenty-fourth day of January, the day when "the sun came back" the first stage of the search ended. And in spite of the number of both dog sled and airplane expeditions which had been carefully and scientifically formed to conduct the search, it was Joe Crosson, who had come first of all, motivated by his friendship for his flying companion, Ben Eielson, and who concluded the search.

On that morning he in one plane and Gillam in another took off from the *Nanuk* about nine-thirty, in fine flying weather. A little after twelve we heard the roar of their motors and saw them circling the ship for a landing. I remember that Marion was the first to get to them. Running toward the plane, she reached it just as Crosson stepped silently from the cockpit, his face set and solemn. The rest of us came up just in time to hear Crosson say, "Well, the search is over."

Then Marion noticed a bundle of crushed sheet metal lying in the cockpit of his plane.

"What's that?" she asked.

"Metal from Eielson's plane," he answered, and all of us turned in silence and walked back to the ship.

The news spread quickly and soon the ship was crowded

with members of the *Stavropol* crew and others who came
from ashore and listened while Crosson told how, just as
we had all suspected, the wrecked plane had been found almost within a stone's throw from the cabin of the Russian
trappers who first reported having heard the motor. Yet,
as near as it was to the searching parties, it was not surprising that it had not been sighted before, in view of the deep
snow and the poor visibility which had hampered the
search. Crosson told us that he would have missed it himself
had it not been that he flew above it during the short time
when the sun was shining for the first day in three months.
What had attracted his attention was the glint of the sun on
the tip of one wing—all that was visible above the snow—
and the shadow cast upon the snow by the wing tip.

As they had approached the trappers' cabin, Crosson, a
little further inland than Gillam, saw the gleam of the
wing. Circling, he had signalled Gillam, who was flying between him and the beach, and they landed on the smooth,
snow-covered ice of a lagoon. Making their way on foot to
the wrecked plane, they had found the cabin inside un-
touched, but the cockpit of the plane was entirely torn
away, and some cases of gasoline, which Eielson had been
bringing to the *Nanuk,* had been crushed by the impact.
But though they had made a long search, they could find no
sign of either of the two men who had been in the plane.

On the face of it, this might have been a hopeful indication. If there were no bodies there, it might have indicated
that the men, having made a forced landing, had managed
to leave the plane and were now safe somewhere, waiting
to be rescued. But there were several elements involved

which made all of us feel definitely that both men had been lost. In the first place, there was every indication that what had happened was not the result of any attempt to make a forced landing, but of a sudden, unexpected crash in a storm. The terrain was such that so competent a flyer as Eielson could have made a safe landing. But the plane was completely wrecked and parts of it were found several hundred feet from the spot itself. Further, the altimeter showed a considerable elevation, indicating the probability that it had been defective and that Eielson may have thought that he was flying at a safe height when his plane hit the tundra at terrific speed. In addition, we all knew that he was thoroughly familiar with the country and if he had left the plane alive, he would have made for the coast and inevitably have encountered the trappers' cabin almost immediately. The fact that he never arrived at this cabin, or made contact with any other human being, convinced all of us that both his and Borland's bodies were lying buried in the snow somewhere near the plane.

We immediately went to the scene with dog teams and men, and began digging. Here and there we found scattered tools, parts of the motor, batteries, seat cushions, and provisions, but no sign of the objects of our search. Meanwhile, the Soviet government sent out digging parties and the Alaskan Airways organized another party. Day after day the long job went on; a week after the digging commenced, Borland's helmet and mittens were found at widely separated points, and any doubt that the men had not met death was completely dissipated.

Since there was nothing further we could do to aid in

uncovering the bodies, Marion and I decided early in February to leave the ship and go back home; pilot Pat Reid offered to fly us to Teller as soon as the weather permitted. On the seventh of February we left the ship, taking with us Captain Milovzorov of the *Stavropol,* who was just recovering from pneumonia and who was badly in need of medical attention.

We landed without incident at Teller, Alaska, and proceeded from there by plane and rail to Seattle. Here Marion, whose newspaper dispatches had been appearing throughout the country, was approached with a number of contracts to go into vaudeville and the movies, but like the sensible person she is, she refused them all and went back to school.

It was not until February nineteenth that the bodies of Eielson and Borland were finally found over two hundred feet from the plane. Both had obviously been thrown out of the cockpit with terrific force and killed instantly. Apparently the terrific wind through which they were flying had blown the plane some distance away from them after it had hurled them to their deaths.

Meanwhile, I had learned what really had happened on November ninth when Eielson had taken off on his fatal flight. He had flown that day as a result of a dare, a taunt flung at him by another pilot, who had accused him of being yellow. He and Borland, in one plane, and Frank Dorbandt and a mechanic in another, had taken off together. They had encountered a terrific blizzard which made safe flying impossible. The two planes were separated and Dorbandt had turned back, but Eielson, apparently smarting under the remark which had belittled his courage, had flown on in weather in which no man should have been in the air. Even under these conditions, however, he had kept his course until the last moment, when probably thinking himself safely in the air, earth and plane had suddenly met in the terrific impact which ended his flight and his life.

CHAPTER XXI

AFTER the two years marked by the freezing in of the *Elisif* and the *Nanuk,* and all the adventures which followed in the wake of these two events, life settled down to a routine of trading which has had little in it worth including in an account of the exciting years Siberia had given me up to that time. During 1931, '32, and '33, I was in and out of Russia, attending fur sales, settling up old accounts, and winding up affairs in general, in preparation for retiring from the active field of Siberian trading. Since then I have been working quietly in my office in Seattle, still in the fur business, but far away from the hazards of the cold, white trail, the squeeze of the ice floes, the filth of a Chuckcho hut, and the gnawing hunger which dogs and men feel during bad winters along the Siberian coast.

But I am far away, too, from the friendly simplicity of the Chuckchos, the hospitality which was perfect and unmixed with any hope for personal gain, the light of loyalty and eagerness in the eyes of my dogs, the pleasures of gossip around an Arctic campfire, the thrill of danger, encountered and narrowly escaped, and the constant pleasant excitement of anticipation from day to day.

Still, I am content. It is all a vivid memory for me still, part of a youth inherited from the strong body of Big Nils and which permitted me to prolong my activities beyond the years which most men call middle-age. I had my fill of life during those years and can live now in the memory of them. Sometimes I get restless, of course, but I can always take a trip to Alaska, or into the Canadian Northwest and fill my nostrils once more with the clean cold wind which has swept over ice and snow. I can tangle my fingers in the hair of some other man's dog, and listen happily to the gossip of trails which my own feet can no longer follow.

But for most of my entertainment I am now forced to fall back upon quieter adventures, finding amusement in contemplating the things which seem important to mankind in civilization, taking my scraps of unexciting fun where I find them, in little ways, as on the day when I was mistaken for the Prince of Denmark.

I was traveling from Vancouver to Winnipeg with three sisters and their husbands, all Russians. I was taking care of the reservations and had wired ahead to Winnipeg for eight rooms, signing the wire simply "Olaf Swenson." When we got into the hotel I heard one of the bellboys whisper excitedly, "Here they are now." Suddenly everyone seemed to burst into excited activity, from the manager down to the smallest of the bellboys. They rushed up to us with an evident air of wanting to give us the hotel, and showed us to the most magnificent rooms in the house.

A few minutes later a bunch of newspaper men came in and wanted a story.

"But there isn't any story," I said.

"There must be," one of them urged. "Why are you here? Why are you traveling incognito?"

Then I began to understand that there was more here than met the eye.

"Who am I?" I asked.

"Why, you're the Prince of Denmark," the reporter answered. "Everyone knows that you were to arrive this morning."

I would have been satisfied with that role, but just then the Prince of Denmark and his party arrived, and I had to give way. Their train came in five minutes after ours. They were going west; we were traveling east. The hotel attendants had thought we were the Prince's party because of the foreign appearance and the charming dress of the women who were with us.

Having corrected that mistake, we unpacked our trunks, and went to the Orpheum Theatre. The next morning, when I was riding down in the elevator, the boy who was operating it looked at me admiringly.

"I saw your act last night," he said, "and it was grand."

"I'm glad you liked it," I said modestly. "What part did you like best?"

"The flying trapeze," he said. "I always like the flying trapeze."

There was a troupe of acrobats at the Orpheum just then, and we had apparently been selected to fill that part. It was quite a come-down after having been the Prince of Denmark the day before, but it was better than nothing, so I let it pass. They never did get us straightened out while we were in Winnipeg.

Well, these little matters are good enough to round out the last years of a life of excitement.

I would not change the past in any particular, not even the worst bumps of the trail or the financial reverses which came with the Revolution and the shifting governments of

Russia. I can think of no life which could furnish greater richness of memory on which to live in one's declining years.

Not that I feel as though I were declining. I still hope to have another crack at Siberia—to see my good friends again, once more to cry "Rapungel?" to them and listen to tales of everything that has happened since I was last there, to feel the joy of traveling behind a dog team with a good leader, and to play again the exciting game of touch and go with a stout ship among the ice fields along the Arctic shores.